MW00795427

"With a distinctive combinatio___
prose, *Maverick Mark* captures ___
It offers striking new insights in ___
domesticated Gospel. Student and teacher alike will learn much when
engaging this stimulating work."

> —John R. Donahue, SJ
> St. Mary's Seminary and University,
> Baltimore, Maryland

"*Maverick Mark* is intentionally—and prophetically—challenging, but
it is also quite delightful. As one who has also experienced appreciation
for this dynamic, even subversive Gospel, I am grateful for Thurston's
powerful communication of these insights to a broad audience in a
moving and memorable way."

> —Elizabeth Struthers Malbon
> Virginia Polytechnic Institute and
> State University (Virginia Tech)
> Author of *Mark's Jesus* and *Hearing Mark*

"In *Maverick Mark*, the reader encounters not only a tightly focused but
a downright urgent guide through the shortest Gospel text. This is a
book that can be given a first reading in a few hours but one its readers
will not quickly forget."

> —Jim Forest
> Author of *All Is Grace: A Biography of Dorothy Day*

Maverick Mark

The Untamed First Gospel

Bonnie B. Thurston

LITURGICAL PRESS
Collegeville, Minnesota

www.litpress.org

1	2	3	4	5	6	7	8	9

Library of Congress Cataloging-in-Publication Data

Thurston, Bonnie Bowman.
    Maverick Mark : the untamed first Gospel / Bonnie B. Thurston.
        p.   cm.
    ISBN 978-0-8146-3552-0 — ISBN 978-0-8146-3577-3 (e-book)
    1. Bible. N.T. Mark—Criticism, interpretation, etc.   I. Title.

  BS2585.52.T47   2013
  226.3'06—dc23   2012046002

*For the Cistercian sisters at
Our Lady of the Angels Monastery, Crozet, Virginia.
Their discipleship is angelic,
and their hospitality embraces imps.*

"Seven times a day I praise you . . ."
(Psalm 119:164, NRSV)

 **Contents**

Hate evil and love good,
  and establish justice in the gate;
it may be that the Lord, *the God of hosts,*
  will be gracious to the remnant.

                    —*Amos 5:15*

Prologue

As I have aged, I have grown increasingly skeptical of taming things. A good deal of what I know with certainty about God (and it is miniscule), I learned from C.S. Lewis' the Narnia Chronicles in which the children are frequently reminded that Aslan (the lion who is the God figure in the saga) is good, but not a "tame lion."[1] Neither is the Gospel tame, although in my darker moods I think the church has spent the last two millennia trying to tame it. This is distinctly odd since the first gospel to be written is not only "untamed," but downright rebellious. To give but one incontrovertible example: what kind of "good news" ends with a fearful silence?[2] I find myself in complete agreement with Annie Dillard's deathless observation in *Teaching a Stone to Talk: Expeditions and Encounters*: "On the whole, I do not find Christians, outside of the catacombs, sufficiently sensible of conditions. Does anyone have the foggiest idea what sort of power we so blithely invoke? . . . It is madness to wear ladies' straw hats and velvet hats to church; we should all be wearing crash helmets. Ushers should issue life preservers and signal flares; they should lash us to our pews."[3] Indeed.

This little book is a modest attempt to "untie" Mark's gospel, to allow its original radicalism to shine forth again and to be proclaimed. That is what Mark's Jesus came to do, not to put down roots and build lovely church buildings (see the chilling Mark 13:1-2) that assist nicely washed and appointed people to maintain the status quo, but to "go on to the neighboring towns, so that I may proclaim the message there also; for that is what I came out to do" (1:38). Jesus' message about the Kingdom of God (*basilea tou theou*) and what it looks like (as opposed to earthly "kingdoms") and Mark's gospel, which records it in Jesus' words and deeds, are shockers. In its tendency to see Mark as the "cookie cutter" for Matthew and Luke, even good scholarship often moves toward "taming" Mark's reality.

I have never quite gotten over reading Morna Hooker's powerful book *Not Ashamed of the Gospel: New Testament Interpretations of the Death of Christ*. The book opens with a graphic evocation of the meaning of crucifixion in the first century. She goes on to explain that the cross was a symbol of weakness and signified total humiliation and degradation. As St. Paul so well understood, the first task of preachers to contemporary Jews and Gentiles was to deal with the problem of Jesus' death.[4] Both Professors Hooker and Robert Gundry (whose commentary *Mark: A Commentary on His Apology for the Cross* was published the year before her book[5]) recognize that "Mark's gospel is a bold apology for the scandal of the cross."[6] Thus from the outset of his gospel with its focus on John the Baptist whose radical preaching led him to martyrdom, Mark continually links the crucifixion of Jesus and what Bonhoeffer so memorably called "the cost of discipleship," thus underlining the truth of the old hymn "if you can't bear the cross, then you can't wear the crown." As Hooker explains, we who wish to share Christ's triumph must share his shame and death. "The belief that God is revealed in the shame and weakness of the cross is a profound insight into the nature of God."[7] Ours is not a tame, predictable or even *reasonable* God, and I, for one, would not worship a God who operated by human reason.

To any way of thinking, a God who voluntarily "un-gods" himself (see Phil 2:6-11) is hardly a "business as usual" God. This understanding of divinity as essentially self-emptying is challenging enough. But as Hooker so succinctly puts it, "His [Jesus'] death is not a substitute, but an exemplar."[8] In Mark's gospel Jesus' authentic disciples play a cosmic game of follow the leader. That an incarnate God dies the most humiliating death possible is ludicrous. That this God invites his disciples to follow suit is incredible. And yet it is exactly what Mark the Evangelist suggests to his audience: take up your cross and follow. As Gundry explains, Mark makes the passion itself a success story.[9] Mark's thought is as wild and untamed as his Greek, which, as any student of Greek can tell you, can be dreadful. A radical message is not about the niceties of grammar in your second language.

Somewhere along the way the wild, unlikelihood of the Christian message, which, let me make clear at the outset, I believe with all my heart, has been reigned in, made to fit more conventional categories of thought. That it is good and moral to be Christian we understand. That it is feral and almost uncontrollably countercultural is something that has been largely forgotten or suppressed. In *Mark for Everyone* N. T. Wright asks the crucial question: "Have we so domesticated and trivialized our Christian commitment, our devotion to Jesus himself, that we look on him simply as someone to provide us with comforting religious experiences?"[10]

In the church of my youth, we regularly sang at the Eucharist these words, the last verse of Isaac Watts' passion hymn "When I Survey the Wondrous Cross":

Were the whole realm of nature mine,
That were a present far too small:
Love so amazing, so divine,
Demands my soul, my life, my all.

As an "older adult," I believe "all" means "all." I do not know specifically what "all" might mean to someone else. I have a pretty clear idea of what it might mean for me—precisely through my study of and prayer with the Gospel of Mark and the very human and incredibly Godly Jesus he portrays. Jesus is not your usual Greco-Roman *kurios*.

When I had finished the rough draft of this book and written about it to my friend M. Marion Rissetto, OCSO, she reminded me of Robert Kysar's 1976 book *John, The Maverick Gospel.*[11] In his very fine work, "maverick" refers to John's literary and theological departures from the synoptic evangelists. Kysar's focus is the religious thought and theological themes of the fourth evangelist. Mine is in the challenges which the first evangelist poses to the typical Christian's and the institutional churches' cultural and economic assumptions, pietized spirituality, and understanding of peace and justice issues.

In what follows, I provide a brief overview of the Gospel of Mark (chap. 1). If you are familiar with Markan studies, you might want to skip this chapter. Then I suggest the gospel's radicality in three areas: discipleship (chap. 2), economics (chap. 3), and what we might call "lifestyle" (chap. 4). This by no means exhausts Mark's untamable message. I do hope it brings that message to bear on practical, personal aspects of every Christian's life and challenges what appear to be common assumptions of churches as public institutions. My work is not prescriptive. I'm not wise (or brash) enough to tell others what they ought to do in response to Mark's gospel and Jesus' invitation to them. (I'm often not wise enough in any given situation to know what *I* ought to do!) But I hope I'm persuasive enough to raise fundamental questions about several contemporary assumptions about Christianity with which, you will see, I disagree. Mark's gospel is never very far away from the cross. If you want happy-clappy Christianity, Mark is not your man. If your doubts can be serious and your darkness can be deep, if you suffer about the serious condition into which the human family has plunged, Mark's portrait of Jesus may well be just what you need to comfort your heart and energize your effort.

And speaking of effort and energy, I am once again profoundly grateful for the work of my colleagues at Liturgical Press who do so much to bring to print and the public my work. Thanks go to academic publisher Hans Christoffersen, and to his staff, particularly Lauren L. Murphy, Colleen Stiller, Michelle Verkuilen, and Barry Hudock. This volume owes a special debt to Professor Amy-Jill Levine of Vanderbilt University who read with great care what I thought was the final draft of the work and made seven pages of thoughtful suggestions. My responses to most of them may not make this a better book, but it certainly makes it a more careful and accurate one. The Rev. Dr. Linda Maloney provided helpful reminders near the end of the process. To those who heard earlier lecture versions of some of this material, I also offer thanks for their attentiveness (or for not snoring if they weren't attentive) and helpful questions.

A number of years ago, the president of the school in which I taught, bemusedly attempting to explain (what we shall kindly term) my quirkiness, referred to me in public (in chapel, no less) as a "maverick." The term may derive from a nineteenth-century American pioneer, one Samuel A. Maverick, who did not brand his cattle. Thus a "maverick" is, technically, "an unbranded range animal," and by extension "an independent individual who does not go along with a group or party."[12] I am "guilty as charged." I think of St. Mark as a maverick in this sense as well, one who was not "toe-ing a party line" but presenting pretty much the unvarnished Jesus story as he received it, early church tradition holds from St. Peter. St. Paul explains that this "passing on" is how the process works. We "pass on" what we "receive," and thus Christianity is both mobile and rooted. (See, for example, 1 Cor 11:23 or 15:3.)

Perhaps, as is often the case with scholars, I found what I looked for. That might be a fulfillment of Jesus' promise in Matthew 7:7 that the searching find. Or it might be a failure of method or intellect or imagination on my part. In any case, there you have it. This is a book about a maverick evangelist by a maverick believer. Consider yourself warned.

Chapter 1

Mark, Gospel of Suffering and Servanthood

The evangelist Mark may be a maverick, but he was not a dis-embodied one. He lived in a particular period of history and wrote for a particular community. Both are crucial to the message and meaning of his gospel. As all theologians do, the writer of Mark had theological and pastoral agendas. His work is historical, but his intentions are not those of a modern biographer or historian. His aim was not to record in chronological order the events in Jesus' life, but to evoke and strengthen faith in Jesus the Christ. The evangelist we call Mark *retells* the Jesus story; his audience certainly knew it at least in outline. James Hoover explains that theologically and pastorally, Mark "sets out to retell the story of Jesus, showing that the kingdom in its glory comes at the end of the path of suffering and service. . . . Mark portrays Jesus principally as the servant-king whom we should follow (Mk 1:17). Thus, if we are to enjoy the glories of the kingdom, we too must follow the road of suffering and service."[1]

While this may sound very stark to modern ears, Mark's was a cru-cial and comforting message for the gospel's original audience which faced persecution for allegiance to Jesus. For them, cross bearing was literal; nobody took up a cross except to go and die. Hideously. To understand Mark's gospel, we must understand the evangelist as a preacher for a specific audience. His, and no other gospel, is "one size fits all." Mark's is a popular work, that is, for the *populi*, the common people, written to strengthen faith in Jesus. Its literary form has affinities with folktales, realistic narratives meant to be told or read aloud. If, as many scholars suggest, Mark wrote primarily for "lower classes" and the marginalized, it means his gospel was first read among "unofficial people" who might well have delighted that nothing good is said in it about "officials," Roman, Jewish, or Apostolic.

Mark's Jesus leads, "goes before"; disciples follow. *Akoloutheo*, "to follow" or "to accompany," is a technical term for discipleship in Mark's gospel which seems more interested in disciples, the wider group of followers, including women, around Jesus (cf. 15:40-41) than apostles (the twelve men Jesus singled out from among them for a particular task). (See 6:6b-13 and 30ff.) The evangelist's reasoning is that if Jesus were persecuted and ultimately crucified (and he was), and if we follow him (and Mark wants us to), how can we expect to escape similar treatment? But if God vindicated Jesus by raising him from the dead (and God did), God will also vindicate us. Mark's is a gospel for a suffering church. That is why it has such power and relevance for today, although perhaps more so precisely among the marginalized and suffering than among "mainline Christians" who are comfortable and "in control."

That, coupled with the historical fact of the death of the eyewitnesses of Jesus' ministry, is why Mark wrote a gospel. Who was Mark and when and where did he write? The most honest answer is that we don't know for sure. The safest (and dullest) answer is that Mark wrote probably for largely but not exclusively Gentile readers (we presume this on the basis of his explaining Jewish customs; see for example, 7:3-4, 19) in the Roman Empire about the middle of the first century AD. In fact, careful reading of the text and scholarship can fill in some of the gaps.

We don't know precisely who the individual person Mark was (or who any of the evangelists were with certainty). "Mark" was one of the most common names in the period. The evangelist probably wasn't the John-Mark of the Acts of the Apostles (Acts 12:12, 25;

15:37, 39) who, in any case, is a man associated with Paul's work (1 Pet 5:13; Col 4:10). It has been suggested that Mark was the "streaker" in 14:51-52 who wrote himself into the story much as Renaissance painters inserted their faces into their paintings.[2] Even if this wonderful, and to my mind fanciful, suggestion is true, it tells us very little about our author. It's fairly clear from the gospel's rough Greek that the language wasn't its writer's mother tongue. And this matter of language raises interesting questions about Mark himself. Was he a companion of Peter, an Aramaic speaker, and himself also a Jew? Or was he a Latin-speaking Roman convert? We don't know.

Ancient church tradition (which, in the interest of full disclosure, I tend to treat more seriously than do some contemporary scholars) almost universally connects Mark to the Apostle Peter. Justin Martyr referred to "Peter's memoirs" in connection with Mark 3:16-17 (*Trypho* 106:3). Eusebius' *Ecclesiastical History* (III.30) quotes an early bishop, Papias (ca. 140 AD) who said Mark was Peter's "interpreter," writing what Peter remembered of Jesus' words and actions, but "not in order." This is important for it means that Mark's ordering of the Jesus material is a primary clue to his intended meaning in any given section of the text. Although many contemporary scholars are skeptical about Papias' report, Justin Martyr, Irenaeus, Tertullian, and Jerome all associate Mark's gospel with Peter, a connection that remained constant well into the fifth century and which is now again accepted by several reputable scholars.[3]

In an e-mail discussion in January 2013 of matters related to this gospel's attitude toward Judaism and to Mark's identity, my colleague The Rev. Dr. Linda Maloney mused as follows: "If we suppose Mark to have been a Gentile proselyte (and not the John Mark of Acts), some ignorance/hostility [toward Judaism] could be explained. Or, contrariwise, if he's just an ardent Jesus Jew, he wouldn't have very cozy feelings about those making the rules for Judaism, either. If he is the John Mark of Acts he's somehow mixed up in the whole fight between Paul and Barnabas and the 'Judaizers' and so on." With the author's permission, I quote from our correspondence to highlight the connection between questions about the evangelist's identity and the attitudes in his work toward the religious tradition of its protagonist, Jesus the Jewish *tekton* (carpenter) from Nazareth.

Scholarly consensus (that rare phenomenon) is that Mark, the first complete gospel to be written, was produced between 65 and 70 AD. The fact that Matthew (sometimes refreshingly referred to as the first commentary on Mark) and Luke use Mark to structure their gospels suggests it came from a city and a major Christian center. Toward the end of the reign of the Emperor Nero (54–68 AD), a thoroughly nasty piece of work, Christians in Rome were subjected to terrible persecutions. Nero (wrongly) blamed them for the fire in the city. With the outbreak of the Jewish War of 66–70 AD, apocalyptic expectations of both Jews and Christians surged (and are clearly evident in Mark 13). Turmoil roils just below the surface of the first gospel.

Both ancient testimony (notably Clement of Alexandria in the second century) and the text of Mark suggest, if not a Roman location for the gospel, at least a location highly influenced by Rome.[4] That the evangelist explains Jewish customs (7:3-4; 12:8; 14:12) and translates the Aramaic words of Jesus that he retains (5:41; 7:34; 15:34 perhaps preserving Peter's aural memory?) suggests he is writing for non-Jews and non-Aramaic speakers. Mark contains Latin loan words though many of them are military terms and could come from anywhere in the Empire. Mark's focal interest in suffering certainly spoke to Roman Christians at the time. While many scholars note strong links to Palestinian Christianity, these would be natural if the first-person memory behind the gospel is Peter's.[5]

Before leaving the matter of the provenance and date of Mark, it is worth noting what C. H. Dodd once highlighted as the three permanent factors in the history of the time. First, there was Rome as the dominant and domineering political order. Second, there were the priests (or Sadducean class, to which I would add the scribes) and Pharisees who represented institutional religion. Finally, there were the Zealots who represented patriotism.[6] Most of the conflict which we encounter in the gospel, and a good deal of its radicality, is connected with one or the other of these three groups. "Politics" is operative on many levels in Mark's gospel.

Why was Mark written? Certainly stories about Jesus circulated before Mark was written, and the contents of Mark suggest the evangelist had access to stories of Jesus' mighty acts. If people heard only these accounts, they would run the risk of understanding Jesus as a magician, engaged in thaumaturgy like the many traveling miracle workers of the time. Similarly, accounts of Jesus' teaching existed before Mark, in particular the hypothetical "sayings source" Q which Matthew and Luke apparently used. If Mark's readers had only that material, they might categorize Jesus as a peripatetic Hellenistic philosopher. Mark wrote for a Christological reason: to help people understand Jesus, *not* who he *was*, because early Christians experienced him, not as a figure from the past, but as a living Lord. This may be Mark's most radical claim. It is certainly one that continues to elicit controversy. Mark carefully arranged Jesus material already in circulation into a narrative that culminates at the cross. Fully a third of the gospel, chapters 11–16, is devoted to the last week of Jesus' life.

Mark suggests that if we want to understand Jesus, we must understand his death on the cross. Mark's focus is the passion of Jesus. This is hard for moderns who tame the cross in fine jewelry to understand. It was hard in the days immediately after Jesus' ascension, as well. In its day, the cross was an atrocious scandal, as Paul makes very clear in 1 Corinthians 1:23: "we proclaim Christ crucified, a stumbling block to Jews and foolishness to Gentiles." Only the most horrible criminals were crucified, a fate reserved for non-Roman citizens, slaves and especially insurrectionists. Crucified criminals were hung naked and left to rot on their crosses, a powerful deterrent to opposing Roman authority. Anyone presenting Jesus to the Hellenistic world had to explain why he was such a wicked criminal who died such an awful death. Mark writes to demonstrate that the Jesus of the mighty acts, the Jesus of the teachings, is the Jesus of the cross. In *Mark: A Commentary on His Apology for the Cross* Robert Gundry argues persuasively that Mark wrote his gospel to explain the shameful way Jesus died.[7] In short, Mark focuses on the suffering of Jesus as *integral* to his identity and mission.

This gives us another clue about why the first gospel was written. Mark wrote for a pastoral reason, to comfort suffering believers. Emphasis on Jesus' suffering points to the fact that Mark's first audience also suffered or anticipated suffering (to my mind further evidence for the gospel's Roman provenance). In the gospel John the Baptist preaches (1:2-8), is delivered up and is martyred (6:14-29). Jesus preaches (1:9-11 and throughout, although Mark records the fewest words of Jesus of the four evangelists), is delivered up (14:10-11) and is martyred (15:1-47). Is this the progression that Mark's community expects for itself? I am disposed to think so. Mark's story of Jesus not only seeks to explain the cross, but intentionally comforts those who follow the Crucified, shows them that their faith in Jesus, their suffering for his sake and the gospel's (8:35) is neither misplaced or without effect.[8] In resurrection, God vindicated Jesus. Mark suggests, albeit subtly, that his followers will receive similar treatment.

Mark was not a modern biographer and did not write to solve historical problems. For him and his community Jesus was a living Lord (and, of course, to call Jesus Lord, *kurios*, was itself seditious), not a figure from history. Mark was apparently indifferent to chronology, and he seems unfamiliar with the geography of Roman Palestine as you will quickly see if you try to plot the travels of Jesus on a map.[9] Although his interest isn't systematic Christology, Mark's concern is theological, to show (and I use the word "show" pointedly, since what Mark wants us to know of Jesus, he tells us by means of the narrative itself) who Jesus is, why he died as he did, and what that death means to his followers. As he addresses those issues, Mark is masterful.

It might be tempting to think that because Mark's gospel is an ancient document, it is "primitive" or not carefully constructed. Nothing could be farther from the truth. Very simply, chapters 1–8 address the question "who is Jesus?" and chapters 11–16, "why did he come?" Mark's structure, that Matthew and Luke basically retain, is geographic: Galilee (1:14–6:13), beyond Galilee (6:14–8:26), Caesarea Philippi to Jerusalem (8:27–10:52), Jerusalem (11:1–16:8). Mark casts Jesus' ministry as a journey to Jerusalem, not as one might expect, the symbol of true religion, but of opposition to Jesus, a point to which I will return momentarily. Jesus leads; disciples "follow." Mark asserts discipleship is learned "on the way" as I hope to demonstrate in the following chapter.

Within the geographical pattern, Mark groups stories by time frame, for example, a day (1:16-39) or a week (chaps. 11–16), and by arranging blocks of similar types (genre) of story, for example, parables (4:1-33), miracles (1:40–2:12; 4:35–5:43; the latter unit demonstrates Jesus' authority over *everything*), or controversy dialogues, stories in which someone tries to "trap" Jesus with a question (as in 1:18–3:6 or 11:27–12:40, a unit of material in which Jesus "bests" representatives of the major parties within Judaism and in Jerusalem). I understand the key to the meaning of any pericope in Mark to be its immediate context in the gospel, what comes before and after the distinct unit. For example, the interpretation of the "widow's mite" (12:41-44) changes when read in light of Jesus' criticism of scribes who "devour widows' houses" (12:38-40).[10] Mark also relies on intercalation, story-within-a-story construction. Perhaps the most dramatic example is the "fig tree narrative" in 11:12-25 in which the temple "cleansing" (11:15-19) is sandwiched between the cursing of the fig tree (11:12-14) and the "return to the tree" (12:20-25). Understanding intercalation helps us interpret the event as a sign act like that of the prophets or an enacted parable rather than an example of Jesus' petulance (although Mark is more likely to describe the emotional state of Jesus than the other evangelists). Other examples of intercalation include 3:20-35 and 5:21-43.

Reference to Jerusalem and the Temple "cleansing" call for a brief excursus highlighting one way Mark is a maverick. In the Jewish popular imagination in Jesus' day, Jerusalem was a "holy city," a repository of a people's memory, site of historical kingship and of the Temple which represented "God in the midst." It was a symbol of God's presence with Israel, of her cultic life, and of forgiveness of sins effected in the Temple by the High Priest on the Day of Atonement. The second Temple, Herod's Temple, was not as large or splendid as Solomon's, but had recently been "redecorated." Herod's work was begun in 20/19 BC and was complete with golden façade by the time of Jesus. It probably did look impressive to Jesus' disciples sitting on the Mount of Olives looking across the valley at it (13:1-3). Jesus was not impressed, and in this he reflected contemporary "fringe" ambivalence about the Temple.

Although the popular view of Jerusalem and the Temple seemed positive (symbol of God's election and Presence), there was a tradition of hostility toward both which is reflected in apocalyptic literature like Ezekiel 40–48, 1 Enoch 83–90, and Mark 13. There was disagreement in contemporary Judaism about Herod's Temple structure (it wasn't built to God's specifications) and cultus (the High Priest was named by the Romans). What we know of the community at Qumran (with whom John the Baptist seems to have had ties) shows it to be critical of the Temple.

From the outset of Mark's gospel, the Temple and its representatives are depicted as Jesus' opponents. (See, for example, 2:1-3:6.) In the account of the "cleansing" of the Temple, only the Markan Jesus adds "for all nations" to the quotation from Isaiah 56:7 (11:17). This can be read as a case in point of the evangelist's general dis-ease with "officialdom." Several scholars, I among them, read 12:38-44 as Jesus' attack on the Temple system which accepted "the whole living" of the most marginalized. Certainly Jesus' condemnation of the Temple in 13:3 seems clear. (Or is it a prediction of what was coming with no judgment implied?) While he suggests that Mark's portrayal of Temple representatives and Jerusalem authorities is not historical but polemical (the reader is to understand them as a composite character opposed to Jesus), J. D. Kingsbury notes that at 15:38, "Jesus supersedes Temple as place of salvation."[11] John Paul Heil argues that the audience of Mark's gospel is to understand itself as replacing the Temple by obedience to Jesus[12] much as Sharyn Dowd's book *Prayer, Power, and the Problem of Suffering: Mark 11:22-25 in the Context of Markan Theology* had suggested that for Christians after the resurrection of Jesus and the destruction of the Temple in 70 AD the spiritual center of gravity shifted from the Temple as a place to prayer, itself as locus of divine encounter.[13]

Mark's Jesus hardly seems "in love and charity" with Jerusalem and the Temple. (Luke paints a rather different picture.) From its beginning his teaching "with authority" (1:22, 27) apparently alarmed the Temple officials (2:6, 3:22). Mark describes their increasing opposition to Jesus whose own stance is either from the beginning anti-Temple (though not anti-Jewish; Jesus is a good Jew who, in fact, argues with Pharisees *like* a Pharisee and loves a man who keeps the law; see 10:17-20), or it becomes so in response to opposition. Vis-à-vis the symbol of Jerusalem and the Temple, Jesus may be the "loyal opposition," like good and faithful church members who call for reforms in their church's structure. But being opposed to the Temple does move Mark's Jesus toward the "fringe." That Mark emphasizes this in his portrayal of Jesus intrigues me because either the Temple and Jerusalem are under siege at the gospel's writing (65–70 AD) or the Temple and Jerusalem are recently destroyed (70 AD) with the utter dislocation this caused both Jewish and Christian communities. Did Mark's original audience watch the triumphal procession in Rome as Titus had the Temple furnishings paraded through the streets as spoils of war (and this indignity later carved for posterity into the Arch of Titus)? And how would this horror and indignity have affected the Jewish attitude toward Jesus, or for that matter, Jewish Christians in Rome of whom Paul's letter to the Romans (and contemporary documents) suggests there were many?

Returning to Mark the literary stylist, the final Markan structural technique I choose to highlight is inclusion, repeating a similar story at the beginning and end of a unit of material to mark it off as a unit, to "frame" it. Mark 8:22–10:52 is the spatial center of the gospel and the heart of its message, and it will be treated in detail in the following chapter. The unit begins and ends with stories about the healing of blind men (8:22-26; 10:46-52). Between these two accounts are three passion predictions of Jesus, each similarly organized and each more detailed than the last. In each prediction story the disciples misunderstand, and Jesus gives further teaching. Everything in the "framed" section is related either to the meaning of Jesus the Christ or to discipleship. The passion predictions point to Jesus' suffering, reinforcing the connection between suffering and discipleship, a central theme in Mark's gospel. The narrative is a journey; Jesus and the disciples are "on the way." They haven't arrived, suggesting that discipleship itself is a process not a "destination" and that a single event in which one "gets saved" was not what the evangelist Mark understood by "discipleship."

Each teaching of Jesus in the journey section stresses discipleship as a matter of servanthood and/or suffering. The suffering of Jesus is linked to the disciples' suffering in the context of service. We will treat this matter in detail shortly. For the moment, suffice it to say that the inclusion of 8:22–10:52 relates the approaching passion of Jesus in the narrative to two problems faced by the community for which Mark wrote the gospel: first, persecution and martyrdom; and, second, the desire for status and domination, a matter that will be examined in the final chapter of this book. To a community suffering persecution and martyrdom, Mark offers an odd consolation: the disciples in his community are to replicate the life of their Lord, and thereby to continue to be close to Him. To a community suffering under the domination of Rome (and prey to the very human urge to power), Mark's Jesus says, "You know that among the Gentiles those whom they recognize as their rulers lord it over them, and their great ones are tyrants over them. But it is not so among you; but whoever wishes to become great among you must be your servant, and whoever wishes to be first among you must be slave of all" (10:42-45). In a society in which many people (some historians believe the majority) were slaves, this must have sounded as radical, and as mad, as it does to us.

At 10:46-52, the closing healing of the discipleship inclusion, an unexpected person, a "nobody on the road of life," confesses Jesus with strongly Messianic titles: "Jesus, Son of David, have mercy on me!" (10:47). The Markan theme of faith from unexpected people (for example, a Syrophoenician woman in 7:24-30 or a centurion in 15:39) is highlighted. Somebody has "gotten it." But to "get it," to understand, is precisely to confess one's blindness and say, "My teacher, let me see again" (10:51). Discipleship is the gradual unfolding of greater insight and following "on the way" (10:52). Jesus now goes up to Jerusalem and its inevitable violence.

Much of Mark focuses on what it means to be a disciple. Matthew and Luke appropriate this theme in their own ways and for their own communities. Ironically perhaps, our maverick Mark depicts unnamed characters, not the Jewish leaders or Jesus' apostles, as exemplars of discipleship: a gentile woman demands inclusiveness (7:24-30); a poor widow gives her life (12:41-44); an anointing woman understands Jesus faces passion and burial (14:3-9). In Mark the "wrong people" (and often female "wrong people") "get it." Mark's portrayal of Jesus' associates, especially the Twelve, is far less positive. They misunderstand Jesus' teachings and Messiahship (4:10; 8:14-21); they are sometimes rude to him (4:38; 5:31; 6:37; 8:4). They clearly don't understand discipleship (8:32) and want to appropriate patterns of power and domination present in their culture but forbidden in the Kingdom of God Jesus preaches and inaugurates. They want to be "the greatest" (9:34), to have the best seats in heaven (10:35-37). Even the women disciples (15:40-41 indicate we must read them back onto the whole narrative), who come off better than the men in the body of the narrative (radical stuff in its day and today in some circles), finally fail to do what they are charged to do (16:1-8), and thus the gospel closes on a note of fear. No disciple is perfect; all are "in process." Perversely perhaps, I take comfort from Mark's picture of the disciples as not only "slow of heart," but downright dumb. If there is hope for them, there is hope for me, and I think that is part of Mark's pastoral point in his depiction of Jesus' disciples.[14]

Of course within the context of Mark's narrative world, the disciples *cannot* understand Jesus. At the outset of the gospel (1:1) and in what I take to be its prologue (1:1-15), the reader is told things that participants in the action of the story don't know. For them, Jesus can be understood only at the cross. The gospel begins with the evangelist's confession "Son of God" (1:1), and closes with the centurion's confession at the foot of the cross, "Truly this man was God's Son!" (15:39). This is another important Markan inclusion, a "frame" closed by another "wrong person," the Gentile executioner. At the moment of Jesus' death, an "outsider" recognizes who Jesus is. As Paul Achtemeier (of blessed memory) so perceptively noted, the disciples couldn't recognize Jesus as King "Until he was enthroned—on a cross; he could not be confessed as king until he had been crowned—with death."[15] This is the central and very ironic point of Mark's gospel, that, to paraphrase Philippians, at the name of one tortured to death on a Roman criminal's cross, one day, not only those who killed him, but all creation *will* bow its knee (Phil 2:6-11). Mark's pastoral point is that in their Lord Jesus all the suffering of disciples finds meaning. In Jesus on the cross Mark's gospel shows us the kind of God we have, and in the process, smashes every idol we have made of God. It may be stark, but it is realistic, and very, very good news.

In the perhaps quirky thinking of the evangelist Mark (although many scholars, I among them, link this theme to contemporary apocalyptic expectation), his audience were participants in a great drama which began with John the Baptist's preaching of repentance and ended with Jesus being raised from the dead. What Marks wants the reader to know about Jesus, he reveals through the narrative itself. Jesus is depicted as the wonder working Son of God, living among people with his human nature evident.[16] In Mark we get an "unsanitized" Jesus, one more likely to reveal his emotions (and I dare to think in some instances, limitations) than in any other gospel. Mark is interested in details and minute particulars and (like anyone writing in a language not his own) prefers the present tense, direct expression which, along with his favorite word, "immediately," moves the story forward to the passion narrative which is his real interest. This realism is calculated to draw us in, to give a "you were there" quality, so that we, too, will follow, will come to learn Jesus "on the way."

Mark frequently calls Jesus "Teacher" (Rabbi), but Mark records few of his words. Except perhaps in chapters 4 and 13 (a Markan framing of Jesus' public ministry), Mark's Jesus doesn't deliver discourses as he does in Matthew and John. Nor does he lay down rules for life in God's Kingdom, although his life and death clearly exhibit two guiding principles: love and obedience. As Stephen Ahearne-Kroll so eloquently puts it, "Discipleship for Mark is not construed as assent to a series of faith propositions or the full acquisition and understanding of divine mysteries. It is predicated on becoming connected with Jesus by following him after his call and acting like him because he is the manifestation of the kingdom on earth. One learns the mystery of the kingdom through the action of following after the one who manifests it."[17]

Mark wants his audience to understand that one is martyred from within as much as from without. This is a powerful message in our self-centered culture. Mark's gospel dramatically illustrates what I take to be the very heart of Christianity on the personal level: that we "find ourselves" in relinquishment of self/ego, in giving self for the other; that life rises from death. Mark's gospel reflects something Joseph Cardinal Bernardin (of blessed memory) said: "It's in the act of abandonment that we experience redemption, that we find life, peace, and joy in the midst of physical, emotional, and spiritual suffering."[18] And as Mark makes clear, even the imperfect and uncomprehending are included in the bargain.

Mark's gospel is about cross bearing as active choice, not passive acceptance. One decides actively to "take up the cross." Cross bearing isn't "putting up with" life's annoyances. This means that suffering is necessarily part of the Christian story, that the relationship of our suffering to that of Jesus' own is somehow mysteriously redemptive for us. And Mark's gospel demonstrates the connections between the personal and the communal, perhaps most dramatically at the close of the gospel when a little community of faithful *and* frightened women are charged to proclaim an astonishing message to a community, "his disciples and Peter" (16:7). That Mark's gospel exists bears witness to that fact that in spite of terror, amazement and fear, they eventually did so.

Mark's gospel is about Jesus, the unconventional One. Christian tradition has rightly characterized Jesus as prophet, priest, and king. At various periods in ecclesiastical history, one or the other image has predominated. I began this chapter with a description of Jesus as "servant-king." But it now strikes me that in Mark's gospel, the figure of Jesus as prophet is paramount. I suggest this in part because of the evangelist's largely negative characterization of the Temple and its functionaries and his equally negative view of "king Caesar" and *his* flunkies. But it came sharply into focus for me in reading a reflection by Anthony J. Gittins, CSSp.

> The sacred figure in biblical literature is not the prophet but the priest. Protected by status, decked in brocaded robes, and privileged to enter the sanctuary, the priest operates within the protective embrace of the sacred temple. By contrast, the prophet is a profane figure. Profane (*pro-fanum*) means "in front of [outside] the temple": that is, dressed in no special garb, quite unprotected, exposed to public scrutiny and ridicule, and subjected to verbal and physical abuse.[19]

Ecce homo! Ecce Deus! Behold the Markan Jesus.

Chapter 2

"Was Blind but Now I See": Discipleship in Mark[1]

Those who follow biblical studies know that particular gospels pass in and out of vogue as objects of scholarly study. There are "Matthean eras" and "Lukan eras" and "Johannine eras." The first decades of the twenty-first century seem to be a "Markan era," having produced several splendid new scholarly commentaries: the long-awaited Hermeneia series volume by Adela Yarbro Collins; the Sacra Pagina commentary *The Gospel of Mark* by John R. Donahue, SJ, and Daniel J. Harrington, SJ; and one by Francis J. Moloney, *The Gospel of Mark: A Commentary;* as well as the two-volume Anchor Bible commentary by Joel Marcus.[2] Happily for preachers, 2002 saw the publication of two books on Mark specifically designed as homiletical helps.[3] There have been a great many other studies focused on specific aspects of Mark, and I would venture to say that the majority of them follow in some way Ernest Best's trajectory by addressing "disciples and discipleship."[4]

As noted in the previous chapter, Mark's is the gospel of the cross and discipleship, and St. Mark was the early church theologian who perhaps understood most fully the profound relationship between the two. It is Mark's Jesus who states unequivocally that anyone who follows him (*akoloutheo* being the technical term for discipleship in this gospel) must take up the cross (8:34). The gospel moves rapidly toward the passion narrative which occupies more than a quarter of it, chapters 11–16. Most scholars agree with Kahler's 1892 observation that Mark is "a passion story with an extended introduction."[5] It is only at the cross that a full Christological confession is uttered, and that by a Gentile centurion (15:39), clearly reflecting the Markan theme of faith found in unlikely persons. Nobody close to Jesus really "gets it" about Jesus until the crucifixion and resurrection, even though the very center of the gospel, chapters 8–10, consists of three passion predictions of increasing specificity and a related series of discipleship teachings.

Many students of Mark have noted that 8:22–10:52 is central to the evangelist's purpose. A parallel commonplace of Markan studies is that, far from being a "primitive writer," Mark is a master storyteller and narrative theologian. Paul Achtemeier observed that Mark collected the Jesus traditions into a story whose order and arrangement would provide the context for understanding and interpreting those stories.[6] I put it less elegantly in the last chapter by saying that what comes before and after a Markan pericope determines its meaning. A primary way we understand Mark's Jesus is carefully to examine the ordering of material in his gospel, his particular redaction.

One of the most carefully ordered sections of a carefully organized gospel is 8:22–10:52. Best points out that "everything in it relates either to the meaning of Christ or to discipleship."[7] This travel narrative in which Jesus and the disciples (a group which 15:40-41 clearly indicates included women) make their way toward Jerusalem is an inclusion framed by stories of the healing of two blind men. As Marie Noël Keller notes, Mark "continues and amplifies the theme of blindness and sight he introduced in 4:1-34 and . . . 8:14-21."[8] In 8:22-26 after what appears to be a false start (more on this momentarily), Jesus heals an unnamed blind man near Bethsaida. Nearer Jerusalem with all its negative associations in Mark's gospel[9] at Jericho Jesus heals another blind man, Bartimaeus (10:46-52). Sandwiched between the two healings of blind men are three passion predictions which are clearly parallel in structure.[10]

The first and probably best-known passion prediction, "Peter's confession," 8:27-38 (although the Matthean version is often recalled for its ecclesial redaction), provides the template. At 8:27 there is a geographical reference, "the villages of Caesarea Philippi." After Jesus' famous questions, "Who do people say that I am?" (8:27) and "Who do you say that I am?" (8:29), there follows the passion prediction (8:31). As representative spokesman for the disciples in Mark, Peter's vehement response (8:32) indicates his (and their) lack of understanding which provides Jesus with an opportunity for further teaching (8:34-38). This pattern—geographical reference, passion prediction, misunderstanding, further teaching—occurs twice more, in 9:30-37 and 10:32-45, as the following chart illustrates:

Geographical reference	9:30; 10:32
Passion prediction	9:31; 10:33-34
Misunderstanding	9:32, 34; 10:35-37
Clarification/further teaching	9:35-37; 10:38-40 and 42-45

In each subsequent instance, the passion prediction becomes more specific and more nuanced until 10:33-34 is, in fact, a nearly complete outline of the Markan passion narrative. Among these passion prediction/discipleship teaching units, Mark has included the Transfiguration (9:2-13) which I take to be an attempt to cure the spiritual blindness of the "inner circle" of Jesus' disciples (Peter, James, and John); the exorcism of a boy with an unclean spirit (9:14-29) which is finally a teaching about prayer and discipleship; an instruction on divorce (10:1-12) which brings discipleship to the homefront; and the encounter of the rich man and Jesus (10:17-31) which indicates, again and in a way we shall treat in detail in the next chapter, the radical nature of economic discipleship.

The section closes with the healing of blind Bartimaeus in Jericho (10:46-52) which I suggested in the last chapter to be a turning point in Mark's gospel. A "nobody on the road of life" calls out to Jesus in Messianic terms that indicate understanding of his identity and mission (10:47-48). "Son of David" indicates who Jesus is and "have mercy" indicates what Jesus came to do. Leaving behind the mantle or outer cloak, symbol of his "work" (begging) and his security (protection from the elements and bedding at night), Bartimaeus goes to Jesus who rewards his faith and his wise request with healing. That healing allows him to become a full disciple; "he received his sight and followed [Jesus] on the way" (10:52). In Mark "follow" "always denotes commitment of some kind."[11]As Earl Johnson has written, "Bartimaeus serves as prototype of the true disciples and provides a model for the Christian who needs to know what it means to see and be saved. After he receives the gift of sight he follows Jesus on the way."[12]

Throughout Mark's gospel the disciples misunderstand the teachings of Jesus. Indeed, as we have noted, they cannot understand them prior to the experience of cross and resurrection. With wonderful subtlety, Mark frames the discipleship section of his gospel with stories of blind men. The lens through which we see discipleship teaching is blindness.[13] In biblical tradition, blindness is negative. God strikes Israel's enemies with blindness (Gen 19:11; Deut 28); blindness is a metaphor for wickedness and foolishness. (See Lev 21:18; 22:22.) In Mark's gospel blindness has to be cured so that discipleship can be understood. This is the "meaning" of the Bartimaeus story. Mary Anne Beavis has reminded us that it was precisely the blind prophet Tiresias who was prescient in Homer and who rightly identified the king's son in *Oedipus*. Bartimaeus is the one who sees clearly.[14] He understands who Jesus is and responds appropriately before (in asking for sight/understanding) as well as after (in following Jesus) his healing.

Bravo for Bartimaeus! But what about the unnamed blind man of Bethsaida? This is a very odd story, one of what I take to be the three most Christologically perplexing pericopae in Mark's gospel. One is the encounter with the Syrophoenician woman in 7:24-30, in my view the key story in the preceding Markan unit which is also "framed," but in that case by feeding stories (6:30-44 for Israel and

8:1-10 in Gentile territory).[15] There Jesus' response to a beleaguered woman is hard to countenance until one reads it as the woman's attempt to cure a certain shortsightedness on Jesus' part about inclusiveness. Jesus "gets it," as his response to the woman (7:29) and his second feeding miracle for those *outside* Israel demonstrate (7:31 and 8:1-10). Mark's third Christologically perplexing scene, the fig tree episode in 11:12-14, I attempted to explain in the previous chapter as part of an intercalation about the Temple. Our maverick evangelist does not shy away from stories that depict Jesus in what seems, at best, shady light.

The difficulty I wish to highlight here in 8:22-26 is not the detail of leading the man out of a village (7:23) or of commanding him not to return to it (7:26, a textually confused verse at best). Both these aspects of the story may be related to what has been called the "Messianic secret" in Mark, that is, Jesus' propensity to say to the recipient of a miracle "don't tell who did this" or in other circumstances, "don't tell who said this."[16] Rather, I have in mind the problem of Mark's picture of Jesus who seems to "flub" a healing (as he apparently insulted the Syrophoenician woman or waspishly cursed a tree for not having fruit out of season). Jesus' "two try healing" is such a conundrum that both Matthew and Luke omit this account from their gospels, perhaps, as D. E. Nineham suggested some time ago, "from a feeling that the use of physical means to effect cures [in this case, spit!] was not consonant with the Lord's dignity."[17] What distinguishes this story from the healing of the deaf and dumb man in 7:31-37, with which it has much in common and in which Jesus, like a good Hellenistic miracle worker, also uses spit to heal, "is the way the cure is effected in two stages . . . and this may have been an additional reason for its omission by Matthew and Luke, if it was taken to imply that the first laying on of hands was not successful."[18]

You see the problem. Why didn't Jesus "get it right the first time?" Why did the blind man first see trees walking and only later have clear vision? Certainly it wasn't the evangelist's allusion to earlier healing literature from Epidaurus?[19] Scholars have suggested a number of solutions to the Christological problem.[20] Perhaps Mark misunderstood or mistranslated the original Aramaic version of the account. Or maybe the man wasn't completely blind when he encountered Jesus. Or perhaps the blindness is symbolic and not literal. Or maybe it's just not that important! Sugirtharajah reads the Markan pericope in light of the "fable of the trees" in Judges 9:7-15, suggesting this is a story about misapprehension of Jesus' Messiahship. While I agree that Mark makes it clear to his readers that "the authority of the kingdom lays in defending the defenseless (sic) and showing solidarity with the weak and needy,"[21] I'm not sure this solves the root problem of "why two tries?"

While I have a tendency to think that the difficulty of the text may well be a mark of the authenticity of its tradition,[22] I admit "immediately" that I do not know the definitive answer to the question posed. Whether Jesus "messed up" the first time and had to double back and "finish the job," or for some reason of his own didn't complete the healing initially is not revealed by the text, and the text is what we have to work with. We could vote on alternatives and determine our majority view, but our vote wouldn't really tell us much historically. For me to presume to know the mind of Jesus when there is no clear scriptural word to reveal or at least give insight into it would be to display a shocking arrogance. So, I can't tell you for sure why Jesus didn't completely heal the blind man with the first dollop of spit and the laying on of hands. I do think I might be able to suggest why the maverick evangelist Mark preserved this story and placed it where he did in his narrative. That is, I might shed some light on the question at a literary, if not an historical level.

I've been suggesting that *arrangement* of the Markan narrative is a key to interpreting any pericope in it. I think the account in 8:22-26 perfectly serves Mark's agenda at this point in the gospel. He wants to illustrate how disciples come to understanding. If blindness is a metaphor for lack of understanding, and I think it hardly requires footnotes to prove that it does in the biblical tradition, then we can "see" that almost everything Jesus says and does in the discipleship section of the gospel (8:22–10:52) is intended to correct partial sight. As are most of the seventeen miracle stories in Mark, this one is intended to impart a theological lesson.[23] The blind man at Bethsaida is representative of the disciples both in their process (gradual coming to understanding) and in the hoped-for outcome of Jesus' teaching (full understanding). And the fact that he fulfills a symbolic function in the gospel does not, in my view, rule out the possibility that he was a "real" blind man healed by Jesus in Bethsaida.

In any case, there are a great many hints that this is what Mark is up to with the placement of this story. First, 8:22 is Mark's first use of the word "blind" (*typhlos*) in the gospel. Unlike Matthew who uses the word frequently in summaries, Mark seems to have "saved it" to use here.[24] It signals that something new is beginning to unfold. Next, recall that Bethsaida means "house of fishers." And who were the first disciples? Simon and Andrew, James and John, fishermen to whom Jesus said, "Follow me and I will make you become fishers of people" ("people" not "men" as the word in 1:17 is *anthropon* not *aner*). And here we are in the home of fisher folk having our vision corrected. In fact, the word is *anablepein*, "to see again," implying lost sight restored, and not only corrected, but perfected. The final adjective in verse 25, *telaugos* (a *hapax legomenon*, a word occurring only here in the New Testament) apparently means "far shining" or "clearly, plainly, distinctly." Donahue and Harrington suggest it "underscores the cure's completeness," and as per their commentary, I wonder if the blind man represents Israel being brought to sightedness about God's Messiah.[25]

Unlike the closing of the "frame" in 10:46-52 where the blind man is named, here the blind man is anonymous. Several scholars have suggested that unnamed characters in Mark (as they are in John's gospel) are to be taken as paradigms or representatives of categories of people. For example, the unnamed woman with the hemorrhage represents those with faith, and the Temple widow represents those who are generous. Mary Ann Tolbert has pointed out that such typological character depiction is characteristic of ancient literature.[26] Here the blind man in the house of fishers is symbolically the disciples: first blind, then partially sighted, and, finally, clearsighted and able to "fish for people." Recall, as well, that "Mark uses 'the disciples' redactionally much more regularly than he does the Twelve."[27] He is more interested in the wider and more inclusive group around Jesus than he is in the Twelve.

With this hypothesis, that 8:22-26, the two-stage healing, is a paradigmatic account, I reviewed the contents of this section of the gospel and found many examples of ways in which Jesus is "correcting partial sight" with regard to discipleship. I can make a case that in the stories in this section of Mark's gospel Jesus attempts to clarify in some way a partial understanding, to make those who see "trees walking," if not perfectly, at least more clearly sighted people. (You might be able to evaluate my hypothesis better if you read these next few pages by following along with your Bible open to this section of the text.) Here I do not try to give full readings of any of these rich passages, only to point out their relevance to the hypothesis.

The first passion prediction unit (8:27-38 or perhaps the account includes 9:1) immediately follows the healing of the blind man in Bethsaida. It opens with questions about who Jesus is. That very exchange is an example of "clarifying" since Jesus first asks who "people" (v. 27 *anthropoi*) say he is, but he really wants to know "who you [the disciples] say that I am" (v. 28). The movement is from the general to the specific, from the "fuzzy" to the "clearer," a process that continues in 8:32-38 in which Jesus tries to clarify Peter's view of what sort of Messiah he is. Peter has it quite right that Jesus is the Messiah, but his understanding is that of "trees walking," as his rebuke of Jesus (v. 32) indicates. Peter needs further work to clarify his sight, and it appears in Jesus' stark teaching about cross bearing (vv. 34-38).

The Transfiguration event that follows in 9:2-13 is part of this process of focusing Peter's, James' and John's (future leaders of the Jerusalem church and the troika of Jesus' "inner circle") view of the Messiah. The three are given a little "preview of coming attractions" as Jesus appears in his glory with Moses and Elijah, representing the Law and the Prophets. The Transfiguration of Jesus, a perplexing and much commented-upon account,[28] is placed here to show the inner circle who Jesus really is. It is followed by an exorcism (9:14-29) in which Jesus' disciples come up short in their attempt to cast out an evil spirit.[29] Jesus must reinforce for the disciples the connection between God's power to heal and their own life of prayer, a connection to which they had apparently been either partially sighted or blind since they had been unable to exorcise the boy. They were correct in trying to cast out the demon (partial sight), but they didn't understand what was necessary to do so and needed further instruction (clarification of sight). This is also a text in which Mark, the evangelist most likely to describe Jesus' emotions, allows the exasperation of Jesus to stand (v. 19). That annoyance, however, does not prevent Jesus from offering further teaching in v. 29.

The second passion prediction unit (9:30-37) becomes an opportunity to heal the disciples' blindness about greatness, inclusiveness, and "little ones" (9:38-50). As with the first passion prediction, the second is followed by further teaching by Jesus to clarify the disciple's sight (v. 35). Jesus draws the circle of inclusion more widely than they would by saying those who aren't against him are for him (vv. 39-41). The stark warnings against leading "little ones" astray apparently follow from the reference to the child in verse 37. In fact, it is interesting to note how often teaching in the discipleship section of Mark has to do with children and "little ones," the powerless and utterly dependent ones in his community. (See 9:14-28, 34-37, 38-42; 10:13-16.) The Jesus of Maverick Mark shows special concern for those to whom others are "blind."

In the conflict dialogue (a story in which someone or a group approaches Jesus asking a question specifically to "trap" or "test" him) centered on divorce which opens chapter 10, Jesus' response attempts to move the Pharisees from "trees walking" to "clear sight." The Pharisees correctly affirm the law of Moses concerning divorce, but Jesus, much as he does in the "antitheses" section of the Sermon on the Mount (Matt 5:17-48), clarifies the motivation behind the law in an attempt to help them understand its full intent.[30]

Perhaps the clearest example of the "sight perfecting" process is Jesus' encounter with the rich man in 10:17-31. The rich man is admirable, but partially sighted. He wants to "inherit eternal life" and has come to ask a rabbi how to do so. He has kept the Law from his youth. His understanding is good so far as it goes, and Jesus "loves him" because he has fulfilled the Torah (10:21). But Jesus also recognizes that his possessions are distorting his vision and offers him a prescription that he cannot fill: "go, sell what you own and give the money to the poor, and you will have treasure in heaven; then come, follow me" (10:21). If the rich man's understanding is flawed, so is that of the disciples who observe the exchange. They think that because the man is rich, he should have been able to fulfill the commandments. That was how it worked. The wealthy could hire out tasks that made them ritually unclean and, therefore, unable to keep the Law.[31] For example, shepherds could be hired to deal with carcasses of unclean animals or workers engaged to sort clean from unclean fish. (See, for example, Leviticus 11.) Tanners of leather had a particularly noxious occupation. The point, of course, is that it is *only* God who is able to make people righteous, "with mortals it *is* impossible, but not for God." (10:27, italics mine). In the pericope Jesus attempts to improve the sight of the rich man (vv. 18-22), the disciples (vv. 23-27), and Peter (vv. 28-31).

In the third and final passion prediction unit (10:32-45) Jesus corrects the partial sight of James and John. That they ask for the "best seats in heaven" is clear indication of their cluelessness and of the evangelist's candor. This question from members of the inner circle of the Twelve is so embarrassing that when Matthew tells the story, he has their mother request privileged seating for her sons (Matt 20:20-28). James and John are correct in their assumption that Jesus can do great things for them. But what they ask is distorted. Ironically, they request the same greatness that was counter-indicated by the second passion prediction teaching, so Jesus must apply again the "spit" of reminder that the one who would be first must be last and servant or slave of all (9:35; 10:43-44). "The rule of discipleship is: Jesus. As Jesus was, so the disciple must be."[32]

In each of these accounts from 8:27 to 10:45, the "picture" of passion and discipleship framed by stories of blind men healed, something partial is completed or some partial sightedness is improved. In the first half of Mark's narrative, there were many examples of the disciples' blindness. They don't recognize who stilled the storm (4:41) or walked on the water (6:49-50). Nor do they understand about the loaves and the miraculous feedings (6:52; 8:17-21). Indeed, the verse that precedes this section of the gospel raises the crucial question: "Do you not yet understand?" (8:21). Obviously, the disciples either don't see, or see partially or distortedly, so in 8:22–10:52 Mark has organized his narrative to demonstrate how Jesus corrects the problem. Ernest Best describes the point as follows: "Mark 8:14-21 is a Markan construction; the disciples are accused of a failure to understand and this failure is expressed in terms of a failure to see. Sight is a widely used metaphor for understanding: Mark 8:14-21 draws this out explicitly. The miracle of 8:22-26 thus represents the restoration of understanding. That Jesus' healing fails at the first attempt and only succeeds at the second represents the coming of understanding in stages."[33]

So far so good. But I would press the significance of 8:22-26 a bit farther. This apparently perplexing story is not only a healing miracle of Jesus which shows how he works with people until their sight (understanding) is clear, but it demonstrates what Mark is doing with the Jesus material from 8:27 to 10:45. Both Jesus and Mark are bringing the partially sighted to full sight. Mark is making it clear that coming to the fullness of discipleship has to do with overcoming blindness, especially the blindness of the disciples themselves and especially their blindness about the mystery of the cross and what it implies for human behavior. For Mark, Jesus' teachings "on the way" bring into focus any fuzziness in the view of discipleship and the cross. And as in many ways Mark's is the most "human" Jesus, I wonder if the increasing specificity of each succeeding passion prediction isn't his indication of Jesus' own "clearing sight."

By 10:33-34 the picture of what is coming for him is in sharp and terrible focus.

Professor Morna Hooker has pointed out that Mark 8:22-26 has an interesting parallel in the account of the healing of the man born blind in John 9. In both, a miracle by Jesus shows "the gradual development of the healed man's faith in contrast to the blindness" of others. John "spells out the parallel between physical and spiritual sight, however, Mark presents it by his juxtaposition of various pericopae concerned with the two themes."[34] Both "coming to clear sight" stories are really about coming to full understanding of Jesus. Mark 8:22-26 is pivotal in Mark's gospel "because it provides a bridge between Jesus' activities in Galilee (1:14–8:21) and his journey to Jerusalem (8:27–10:52) and sets the theme and tone of the journey narrative: the need to come to understand the teaching and healing activity of Jesus in light of the mystery of the cross."[35]

In a very lucid and persuasive article to which I was directed after I had organized my thoughts on this section of Mark, "Opening Blind Eyes: A Revisioning of Mark 8:22–10:52," Marie Noël Keller notes that the two blind men that frame it are metaphors for Mark's community.[36] The unnamed man represents their present faith. Bartimaeus is what Mark hopes for them. (The two healed blind men are like "before" and "after" photos seen in ads for diets and body building.) Within this frame, Mark uses the well-known rhetorical device of example to show his community what they need to learn in order to change and perfect their attitudes and behavior. Keller suggests the Markan community needs "to acknowledge that their initial profession of Jesus' Messiahship is inadequate," to "accept the fact that following Jesus involves sharing in his suffering," to "pray for the faith that they need in order to trust God's plan," and to believe that Jesus "will give them 'clear eyes' to see the path they must follow."[37]

If my theory and Keller's about why Mark included 8:22-26 at this point in his narrative is accurate, it may also shed a tiny ray of light on one of the other puzzles in the gospel, the presentation of the disciples as uncomprehending. It has for some time been a "given" of Markan studies that the disciples are "dummies"; they "don't get it." But, as David Hawkin notes, Mark's *purpose* for that characterization was neglected until the mid-nineteenth century.[38] What more recent scholars have come to understand is that Mark's characterization of the disciples is a teaching device, a pedagogical ploy. What the disciples don't understand highlights what Mark wants his readers (the disciples in his own community) to be clear about. The disciples in the gospel are first portrayed positively so that the reader identifies with them. But their characterization gradually turns negative. (Perhaps this is another indication of the independence of Mark's approach to the Jesus material.)

R. C. Tannehill explains that the reader is led in the first chapters of Mark to view the disciples positively, to have high expectations for them. They have "followed" Jesus, responded to him, bonded with him. Although there have been indications of their obtuseness, beginning with the feeding of the five thousand (6:30), the characterization changes; the disciples fall into "ill repute" as they are constantly depicted as uncomprehending, unable to see and hear. Having eyes, they do not see, and having ears, they do not hear (8:8). This incomprehension reaches its height when, at Gethsemani, they abandon Jesus altogether. Tannehill suggests the disciples are foils to Jesus. The reader judges them in light of what Jesus says and does. Mark hopes we will identify with the disciples, see their failures as our own and thus be called to repentance[39] and clear sight.

A slightly different reading is provided by J.F. Williams who argues that the increasingly negative presentation of the disciples is intended to lead the reader to identify, not with them, but with the minor characters of the gospel.[40] Increasingly, it is the minor and often unnamed characters who exhibit true discipleship.[41] A nameless woman made ritually unclean by a gynecological problem becomes a paradigm of faith (5:25-34). A Syrophoenician woman calls Jesus to a more complete understanding of who is included in the Kingdom (7:24-30). A nameless blind man is brought to full sight (8:22-26). A nameless widow is the example of generosity, of "giving the whole life" (12:41-44). A nameless woman performs the prophetic ministry of anointing Jesus (14:3-9). A nameless centurion (for heaven's sake!) confesses Jesus (15:39). You see the pattern? And notice how many of these nameless exemplars are female, certainly a "maverick" touch.

One of the reasons I think Mark's Jesus commands the disciples (and others) not to proclaim his Messiahship is that they don't yet really understand it.[42] They shouldn't teach what they don't understand (which is a good pedagogical principle I wish all my teachers, and I myself, had followed). The imposition of secrecy is not permanent; at 9:9 Jesus says it only holds "until the Son of Man should have risen from the dead," thus highlighting the importance of the cross and passion, which Mark mentions explicitly at least five times in this unit of material. As Eduard Schweizer so eloquently wrote, Jesus cannot be understood without the cross. Divine Sonship shows itself primarily in rejection, suffering, dying. And only one who follows Jesus on the way of the cross will be able to experience the power of his signs and miracles.[43] And, I would add, understand clearly that to which they point.

In this most important matter Jesus doesn't want the "blind leading the blind" as it were. Mark apparently understood this. "By placing 8:22-26 at the beginning of the journey narrative Mark has imbued the story. . .with symbolic or spiritual value. It will take time for Mark's readers to absorb the idea of Jesus as the suffering Messiah."[44] So at the spacial center of his gospel, after the reader has begun to doubt the disciples and admire the nameless minor characters (*not* the religious authorities, *not* the Twelve or those close to Jesus and certainly *not* Roman officialdom), Mark places the story of a nameless blind man whom Jesus, in stages, brings to full sight. The pericope is a cameo of what the whole gospel of Mark is doing: bringing fuller understanding to those who, in the words of St. Paul, "understand in part" (1 Cor 13:12). And Mark's gospel is a cameo of what Jesus is still doing: bringing us all, and especially we "nameless ones," to full sight.

As Francis Moloney points out in his engaging commentary on Mark, Jesus' rebuke of the disciples in 8:17-21 prepares for the miracle story in 8:22-26. The question is, "do you *not yet* understand?" (8:21, italics mine). There is a ray of hope that at some point, the disciples might, indeed, understand. "There is hope that they may still move from the blindness of their unfaith into true sight. The miracle story of 8:22-26 is a paradigm of that possibility, and plays an important literary function in setting the agenda for the rest of the Gospel."[45] Sight does, eventually, come, but only to those who continue on the way that leads to the cross. Enlightenment comes on the other side of the cross in the Easter dawning. But in Mark's gospel, even then, full understanding is tenuous as 16:1-8 makes, well, *clear*.

That is the point at which what Mark is doing in 8:22-26 becomes the Good News for us. As Donahue and Harrington observe, "most of us can identify with the experience of faith as a gradual process in which sometimes things look blurry and at other times we come to see clearly."[46] We may not be able to see the forest for the trees. Indeed, the trees themselves may not be very clear to us. But Jesus does not give up on his myopic disciples. He spits and touches, spits and touches as we make our journey from no sight, to partial sight to full sight, from imperfect discipleship, to cross, to resurrection.

And note in closing that the *initiative* of Jesus in all this is a very subtle way in which Mark addresses that fundamental theological idea, grace, and the ongoing Christian misunderstanding of it, that somehow we can "do it ourselves." The matter of grace, which is really the human problem of the inability (and often unwillingness) to abandon ourselves, to surrender to what God's love alone can do in and for us, was of great concern to Paul writing to the church in Rome, the same church to which, some years later, I think Mark's gospel was addressed. After discussing his lack of understanding and inability to do even what he *does* want to do vis-à-vis the Gospel (7:15-23), Paul exclaims, "Wretched man that I am! Who will rescue me from this body of death? Thanks to be God through Jesus Christ our Lord!" (Rom 7:24-25). This is the very point Mark's Jesus made to Peter and the disciples: "For mortals it is impossible, but not for God; for God all things are possible" (10:27). All things are possible (but not guaranteed!) for those who give up trying to do it all for themselves and surrender to what God has done in Jesus Christ. That is the radical grace which the maverick gospel of Mark offers, and by that grace, we who once were lost are found. We who once were blind will see.

Chapter 3

Mark and Economic Justice[1]

This chapter explores the possibility that Mark's gospel reflects a discernible interest in what we call "economic justice."[2] There is a substantial amount of necessary preparatory material to consider before we can enter the world of the gospel and its economic realities and attempt to discover Jesus' teaching. But first, I want to introduce two caveats before sketching something of the historical-economic background of Mark's gospel and then highlight some passages in Mark which shed light on the evangelist's "Kingdom economics."

Caveats

First, to be honest, I don't think St. Mark consciously set out to write about what we call "social justice," which is really a modern concept. Nor did Jesus affirm or excoriate a particular economic system and certainly not one that didn't exist in the first century. As previously suggested, Mark wanted the first recipients of his gospel to understand who Jesus is, not was, because Mark understood him to be a living Lord, not an historical figure from the past. What sort of Messiah is Jesus? And how is that related to his audience's experience? These are Mark's questions (and those of any good interpreter of the Jesus tradition). Mark's intent was to show that Jesus is the suffering Messiah, the King on the Cross, and to communicate that to a community facing persecution. What Mark says about "social justice," he says to the persecuted. I suggest his community's persecution was economic as well as religious. Additionally, Christianity was *religio illicita*, an illegal religion, in the Empire until the time of Constantine.

Nevertheless, Mark's report of the action and words of Jesus is noteworthy and good news to the economically oppressed and depressed. Nothing that Mark writes about those with power, whether that power is religious or social or political or economic, is very positive. In Mark's gospel, Jesus is most enthusiastically received by those on the margins: the poor, the unacceptable, the radically "other," women, the sick, and the crippled. Indeed, the fullest confession of who Jesus is, is made by the enemy executioner: the Roman centurion (15:39). We might pause to think about the contemporary implications of this for us in light of Thomas Merton's insistence that "We must find [God] in our enemy, or we may lose him even in our friend."[3] Also relevant is the fact that many of our churches are very much part of the structures of power and privilege in our society.

Second, the English word "justice" may not be the correct term for what we are considering in this chapter. The more biblical and accurate term might be "righteousness," *dikaiosune* in Greek. The first definition of this noun is "what *God* requires" (italics mine) and of the verb form, "put into a right relationship (with God)."[4] This is an important distinction because in English "justice" is a legal or juridical term. In Greek "righteousness" is a theological and relational term. The issue is what God wants, not what is "fair" or "just" from a human perspective. "Whereas in English *justice* emphasizes conformity to a society's standards, *righteousness* usually denotes conformity to God's standards or religious norms."[5] Practically, this means that there is little point in insisting on justice in a society whose standards are morally disordered and theologically bereft. As Scot McKnight so succinctly puts it, justice "generally expresses conformity to God's will in all areas of life: Law, government, covenant loyalty, ethical integrity or gracious action. When humans adhere to God's will as expressed in his Law, they are considered just or righteous."[6] The standards toward which we strive must be none less than those Jesus teaches when he speaks of the *basilea tou theou*, the Kingdom (or reign) of God.

When the New Testament uses the term translated into English "justice," it doesn't usually mean equal treatment under the law but conformity to the will of God. Its implication is spiritual not legal. As such "justice" would not be legislatable, except in a theocracy (not to put too fine a point on it, the sort of government with which America has been so uncomfortable in the Middle East). In light of the death and resurrection of Jesus Christ, what Christians are called to live by is not justice but mercy, not settling for "tit for tat," but first accepting and then striving to live the mercy and loving kindness of God.

Jesus' atonement reflects God's grace and effects mercy not justice. The letter of James says simply "mercy triumphs over judgment" (2:13). I would suggest that justice is what we want for *other* people; mercy is what we want for ourselves. Jesus says we must "do unto others" as we would want to be "done unto" (Mark 12:30-31). So our primary mode as Christians is not first the "doing" mode of justice, but the "receptive" mode of grace and mercy—from which our action should then spring. We are to respond to others in the knowledge of being the recipients of God's grace. If we are not acting from the *koinonia*, the community of "saved sinners" (to put it crudely), we are very likely "doing unto" others, treating them as objects and as other—both grave spiritual failings.

This is an important theological point as we turn to "maverick Mark's" portrayal of Jesus' teaching (albeit oblique) about economics. "Justice" is a legal term; "grace" and "mercy" are theological terms that lead us to live relationally in ways more appropriate to life in the Reign of God. And the Reign of God is the standard against which we must measure any society's treatment of people, but especially the most vulnerable members of society. Indeed, societies are most clearly revealed by the condition of their most vulnerable citizens. As I hope to demonstrate, these points are the tap roots of Jesus' "Kingdom economics."

Backgrounds

To understand what Mark's Jesus suggests about economic righteousness, how we might live together as if we really believed we were God's family as defined by Jesus in Mark 3:31-35 (especially v. 35), we must enter the ethos of the first-century Roman Palestine (see chap. 1, note 5) and know something of its historical setting and economic environment.

Historical Setting

The historical background of Mark's gospel (and thus of the evangelist's thinking) begins in the fourth century before Jesus when the westward expansion of the Persian empire led to clashes with the Greeks, and Alexander the Great set out on a military and cultural quest that enveloped the ancient (largely western) world. The aims of Alexander were cultural as much as military; he wanted a Hellenized world. "Hellenism" is the term for the cultural program of the Greeks as they expanded their geographical territory.[7] Hellenism posed a direct threat to Judaism because the great rational and ethical achievements of the Greeks (not to mention their artistic traditions) made the radical demands of obedience to YHWH appear to be naïve. In addition to the fact that Hellenism gave us the language in which the New Testament is written, it presented a threat to Judaism which we might properly call the threat of secularism. The First Book of Maccabees presents the difficulty from the Jewish point of view. The problem is cultural imperialism imposed on a subject people. (This sounds eerily familiar.) To make this long and interesting story short, after a period of guerilla warfare, in 165 BC the Jews threw off their Greek occupiers and established an independent, Jewish state under the Hasmonean dynasty of kings and queens.

This second, independent Jewish kingdom lasted about one hundred years until 63 BC when as a result of civil unrest the Roman General Pompey placed Jewish territories in the Roman province of Syria under a puppet king. When Marc Antony came to power in

42 BC, he put Herod the Great on that throne. Herod ruled from 37 to 4 BC and left things in such a state that in AD 6 Rome placed Judea under the direct rule of a governor, a procurator, who ruled from Caesarea Maritima and only came to Jerusalem during pilgrimage festivals (like Passover) to help keep the peace. This situation lasted until AD 66 when full-scale revolt like that at the time of the Maccabees erupted. But this time the Jewish fighters were no match for the legions of Rome which crushed the rebellion and destroyed Jerusalem and the Temple in AD 70. This catastrophic event is the immediate context of Mark's writing.[8]

The point for us is that with the exception of about one hundred years, Israel was under military occupation or political domination by other empires with other cultures and especially other religious views. When we think of "justice" in connection with the New Testament, we must think of it in relationship to a subjugated people under Roman control. One sees this reflected in other gospels as well as in Mark. For example, in Matthew's gospel Jesus alludes to the Roman soldier who could force someone to carry his luggage for a mile (Matt 5:41). Paying taxes to Caesar about which Jesus is cross-examined in Mark 12:13-17 reflects political domination since one of the great oppressions of Roman occupation was economic in the form of taxes. In order to understand this, we need to know a bit about economics in Roman Palestine.

Economic Environment[9]

As John Stambaugh and David Balch point out in their book, *The New Testament in Its Social Environment*, for "Greeks, Romans, and Hebrews . . . wealth and status were measured in terms of lands or flocks."[10] While money/coinage and moveable wealth were factors in New Testament times, basic wealth was agricultural, and thus "material wealth of the Greco-Roman world was distributed unevenly. A tiny fraction of the population owned a vast proportion of the land and resources, and the mass of men and women had to make do . . . or scrape by on very little."[11] (Once again, depending on your circumstances, this can sound very contemporary.) In a fascinating article on the social location of the Markan audience, Richard Rohrbaugh provides the following statistics: 2 percent of the population were "urban elites" (including high military officers, priestly families, and Herodians) whose wealth was built on land ownership (1 to 3 percent of the population owned the arable land) and taxation; "urban non-elite" (merchants, artisans, day laborers) were 5 to 8 percent of the population; "degraded, unclean, expendable" (beggars, prostitutes, laborers) were 10 percent of the population; most of the population lived in villages and rural areas and were peasants at minimum levels of survival.[12]

The majority of the Greco-Roman workforce was engaged in farming and herding; for most of them economics was subsistence, hand to mouth, day to day.[13] These are the people who were prominent in "Mark's story world," the *ochlos* (the crowd, a term used thirty-eight times in Mark).[14] We know from the synoptic parables of Jesus that many workers were hired by the day, and whether their families ate depended upon whether or not they were paid. (See, for example, the "Workers in the Vineyard" parable, Matt 20:1-15.) In classical literature the "poor man who had to work with his hands and hire himself out at the behest of another was regarded with disgust rather than pity. . . . The notion that the poor were in some way 'blessed' (Matt 5:3; Luke 6:20) would have struck as preposterous anybody raised in the aristocratic circles of Greco-Roman society."[15]

Other ways of making a living than by agriculture are reflected in Mark's gospel. In coastal areas there was fishing, but the cost of the equipment was high. The fact that James and John leave their father Zebedee in the boat with the hired servants (Mark 1:20) suggests that they were not poor, but something like middle-class, small-business owners with "business capital" and employees. As we know from other gospel stories, the living of fishermen was uncertain; not all fish bite (a circumstance to which "fishers for people" can also relate).[16] Manufacturing was done on small scale to meet local need; potters, weavers, blacksmiths, carpenters were small-business owners and catered to local clientele.[17] St. Paul the "tent maker" was of this sort, but the fact that he calls attention to work with his hands suggests that he wasn't born to it, but took it up of necessity.

The basis of the economy was agricultural, but by Roman times, the population was moving toward urban centers, and from this many difficulties arose.[18] Cities grew up as trading centers, centers of Roman administration, of religious practice, and places of pilgrimage. The wealthy had agricultural estates but lived in the great cities of the Empire, renting out their lands for farming or putting them under managers. Several synoptic parables of Jesus reflect the situation of wealthy landlords who entrust their property to stewards. (See Matt 21:33-41; 25:14-20.)

Wealthy people provided the market for luxury goods like silks and linens and fine dyes, oil and wine and perfumes, and, of course, precious metals and gems. "Conspicuous consumption was a required life-style of the upper classes; wealth functioned as a proof of social and political status."[19] Slaves constituted another aspect of wealth. Dealers and brokers could make good money from the slaves who might be highly educated captives from war or in debt slavery, another fact reflected in Jesus' parables (Matt 18:23-35). Teachers, cooks, physicians, and managers were often slaves as well as those who did the physical work at the baths, mines, and farms.[20]

"Most commercial activity in the Roman empire was local."[21] "Banking" was often a matter of burying your coins in a field and hoping nobody else bought it (Matt 13:44 and compare Matt 25:25). Operations that modern banks perform were functions of social relations: one borrowed money from friends who might prove not to be so friendly when they bound the debtor into bondage or slavery or prison for debt. Debt was such a social problem that during the Jewish revolt of AD 66 to 70, the common people burned the debt records in Jerusalem.[22] Money changing was hardly a laudatory occupation since in addition to collaboration with the Romans, the possibility for graft and corruption were great. These facts account for some of Jesus' anger in Mark 11:15-19, especially verses 15 and 17. But money changing was important in Roman

Palestine since the Temple tax had to be paid with Tyrian shekels and Roman taxes with Roman or other coinage.[23]

This introduces two final aspects of economic life in Mark's world: coinage and taxation. With such an extensive empire, the Romans had to depend upon standardized coinage. We know from the parable of the woman and her lost coin (Luke 15:8-10) that money was important in rural Palestine. "The standard silver denomination was the denarius, known in the East by its equivalent in Greek, *drachma*. The parable of the vineyard (Matt 20:1-16) implies that a denarius was a generous day's wage for agricultural workers."[24] Mark 6:37 estimates that bread to feed five thousand would cost two hundred denarii. To give some idea of what that meant, soldiers in the Roman legions of the first century received 225 denarii per annum; auxiliary and less elite troops, much less. Ordinary, daily transactions were in bronze coins, known as *as* or *assarion*. A denarius was worth sixteen *asses*. Matthew 10:29 says two *asses* buys four or five sparrows. There were even smaller coins like the *lepta* of the widow's "mite" in Mark 12:42.

Perhaps the principal use of coinage in the world Mark describes was to pay the taxes that funded the Roman Empire and the Temple in Jerusalem. "Jews in the time of Jesus were subject to a complex system of religious and secular taxation."[25] When Rome annexed Judea in 63 BC, the High Priest was responsible to pay a tribute tax to Rome and that tax was exacted from the people. This is another reason why in previous chapters I pointed out that Mark's gospel is less than enthusiastic about Jerusalem and the Temple functionaries. The half-shekel Temple tax (Neh 10:32-33) was for maintenance of the Temple and its personnel in Jerusalem. One source of irritation in connection with the payment of the Temple tax was that the "priestly aristocracy belonged to the wealthy class."[26] (Like so much that seems familiar here, it seems ubiquitous that the privileged, educated, and rich tax the poor.)

Helmut Koester notes that "the primary source of income for the imperial treasury . . . was from taxes, which came primarily from the provinces. Roman citizens . . . were exempt from direct taxation."[27] Roman taxes were of three kinds. First, there was a land tax (*tributum soli*—note the word "*tributum*," a reminder that taxes were "tribute" owed by vassals to overlords) on the produce of the land. This tax was enforced whether or not the land produced, so it was a real threat to subsistence farmers. City residents paid a house tax. Second, a head tax (*tributum capitis*) was levied on males aged fourteen to sixty-five based on periodic census data (like the one alluded to in Luke 2:1-5). This was expanded to include women. (Kudos for equal rights!) Mark 12:13-17 discusses whether Jews should pay this tax. Third, Rome instituted a very complex system of customs duties collected at ports and city gates which varied from 2 to 5 percent of the value of goods transported. The tax collector friends of Jesus may have collected this revenue. Also, in some parts of the Empire there were heavy sales taxes.

Tax collectors for Rome were notorious for their dishonesty (thus the synonymous "tax collectors and sinners" in our gospels) and were hated as collaborators. They were considered quislings.[28] It is noteworthy that one of Jesus' chosen Twelve was Levi the tax collector (Mark 2:14). In calling the Twelve, Jesus constituted an extremely interesting and varied group. There was genuine "diversity" when a tax collector, perhaps a Roman employee, was expected to work and live with a Zealot, what amounted to a first-century terrorist committed to getting Rome out of Jewish Palestine by any means. (See Luke 6:15.) When the gospels speak of taxes, we must remember that they were not only an economic burden but "a painful symbol of conquest."[29] On the basis of Josephus' reports, it is estimated that at the time of Herod, "the average man worked about three weeks per year for the state. For those who lived close to the edge of poverty. . .there were many who did—this amount would be felt as a heavy burden."[30] One scholar thinks that the joint taxation by the Romans and Tetrarchs exacted a total burden of 49 percent of a person's income.[31] Another scholar puts the figure at between 30 and 70 percent.[32] With these sobering statistics in mind, we turn to address the issue of economic justice as it plays out in Mark's gospel.

Economic Justice and Mark's Gospel

Socio-economic Circumstances in Mark

While I think Mark's audience is a predominantly Gentile community in the second half of the first century AD, probably in the wealthy city of Rome (and thus perhaps the same to which St. Paul addressed Romans), the *setting* of his narrative of Jesus and the disciples is rural Roman Palestine at the outset of the century. In his book on poverty in the Bible, Leslie J. Hoppe writes:

> Jesus and his disciples were not among the elite of Roman Palestine. They shared the lot of the poor. Though the disciples worked as fishermen, their labor barely provided enough to keep them from destitution. Their profits were diminished substantially by Roman taxes and Jewish tithes. . . . Throughout his life Jesus was able to dissociate himself from possessions because they accounted for nothing in terms of the reign of God that he was called to announce. He challenged his followers to trust in God implicitly. . . . His solidarity with the poor became complete during his passion, when he died the death of a criminal.[33]

The Gospel of Mark reflects a range of economic circumstances. Although Roman cities were culturally dominant, some 90 percent of the population lived in villages and rural areas, most peasants at bare survival level.[34] There were beggars like blind Bartimaeus in Jericho (10:46-52) and the infirm and crippled—the leper (1:40-45), the paralytic (2:1-12), the man with a withered hand (3:1-6), the Gerasene demoniac (5:1-20), the woman with the gynecological problem (5:25-26)—all those whose circumstances or infirmities prevented them from making a living. Many healing miracles of Jesus reflect the state of health as well as economic condition of the poor. Restoration to health was also restoration to economic productivity.

The rural poor included most of the five thousand in Galilee (6:30-44) and the four thousand in the Decapolis (8:1-10) upon whom Jesus has compassion because they don't have any food with them. (Jesus' disciples were not so tenderhearted.) In 8:2 Jesus ex-

plicitly says, "I have compassion for the crowd, because they have
been with me now three days and have nothing to eat." The crowds
who followed Jesus were apparently hand-to-mouth people, those
who sought food day-to-day, subsistence folks always on the edge.
The feeding miracles suggest that hunger was the normal condition
of many (in contradistinction to our society in which overweight
is). That Jesus' disciples pick grain on the Sabbath and that Jesus
defends the action suggests they, too, were occasionally hungry
and not carrying provisions (2:23-28). Indeed, Richard Rohrbaugh
argues that the rules Jesus breaks are the ones peasants had the most
difficulty keeping.[35] When Jesus sends the Twelve out on mission,
he commands them to join the hungry of the feeding stories by leaving behind provisions ("no bread, no bag, no money in their belts"
[6:8] and depending on local hospitality which might, of necessity,
be very thin, indeed [6:17-23]). Perhaps it is not too strong to say
that Jesus asks the shepherds to share the poverty of their sheep.

At the other end of the spectrum, Mark's gospel reflects wealth
and position. The tax collectors in 2:13-17 were probably comfortable. They certainly had access to money. In Mark 7 Jesus is
especially critical of scribes and Pharisees who came down from
Jerusalem, the center of religious wealth and power, and whom he
accuses of not discharging their economic and, more pointedly,
human responsibilities (7:9-13). The Herodians were, as the name
suggests, politically aligned with the House of Herod and thus more
likely to be well to do. In chapter 5 Jairus, he of the dying daughter,
is a ruler of the synagogue, possibly a position of economic as well
as spiritual achievement as "rulers" were often "patrons" as well.[36]

On the way to Jerusalem, Jesus meets a rich man whom Mark
says "had great possessions" (10:22). His inability to divest himself of them leads to one of the few explicitly economic statements
of Jesus, "How hard it will be for those who have wealth to enter
the kingdom of God!" (10:23; note that this is not impossible but
hard). Peter, often spokesman for the disciples, is appalled because
he knows it is precisely the wealthy who could hire others to do
the ritually defiling work, who thus were "clean" for the religious

observance that made one cultically "righteous." (See chap. 2, note 31.) A remark by Albert Nolan is relevant here:

> To appreciate something of the impact that such a reversal must have had, we might imagine someone who goes around today telling the rich and those who have a high standard of living that they are not blessed, that in fact they are the most unfortunate. Why? Because the only way the human race can survive will be for the rich to lower their standard of living and share their wealth with others. The rich are going to find that very difficult.[37]

In the parable of the sower, the thorns that choke out the seed/word are "the lure of wealth, and the desire for other things" (4:19). Jesus was speaking to some among his disciples in Galilee, or at least reflecting a reality they would recognize (4:10, 33-34). But generally Mark compares the rural poverty of those in Galilee and the Jordan Valley with the life of the elites in Jerusalem and with the Roman retainers. As previously indicated, Mark is skeptical of both groups. The authority figures whom Jesus encounters in Jerusalem, especially the high priest and his associates, and Pilate and his court, were all wealthy—wealthy enough to buy Judas' betrayal (14:11). Joseph of Arimathea, a member of the Sanhedrin and thus a person of prestige, had money for both a linen shroud (linen was a luxury fabric) and a rock tomb (15:43-46).[38] Overall, however, unlike Luke's Jesus who is more gentle in his treatment of the rich, Mark's Jesus tends toward criticism of the rich, especially those who are attached to their wealth at the expense of the Kingdom's invitation. The difference probably originates in the two evangelists' audiences.

Somewhere between the two extremes of abject poverty and wealth are Jesus himself and his disciples, the smaller group of the Twelve, and Jesus' "inner circle" of Peter, James, and John. Wilfred Harrington points out that Jesus "had a free attitude toward property. He took for granted the owning of property. In the setting of his Galilean village . . . property would be modest indeed. He himself was a tekton, an artisan . . . a village tradesman."[39] It could be that Jesus owned or rented a house in Capernaum. Some manuscript traditions of Mark 2:1 read he was "at home," and in 2:15 "in his house" (*en te oikia autou*). Yet when Jesus began his public ministry, he left his trade behind and became dependant on the generosity of others: "during his itinerant mission, he had no possessions. And he did, with severity, attack wealth where it had captured people's hearts and had blinded their eyes to God's purpose. He had surplus wealth in mind: the rich ought to use their wealth to benefit the poor."[40] That Jesus understood the difficulty of this is conveyed by the metaphor of the camel and the needle's eye in Mark 10:25.

Jesus' "inner circle" may have approached something like middle class. The fishermen James and John owned a boat and had hired help (1:16-20), and perhaps for this reason *could* accept Jesus' invitation to follow. Peter and Andrew apparently owned a home (1:29) and could leave at least that to a wife, mother-in-law, and family members. As noted, Jesus, himself, may have had a house in Capernaum. Certainly he is called the "carpenter, son of Mary" (6:3). "Carpenter" (*tekton*) suggests an artisan, indicating his status as a tradesman, and "son of Mary" his uncertain parentage. Levi the tax collector certainly had access to money (2:14). Of the economic status of others among the Twelve, we know nothing, except that Judas had his price.

Mark is generally more interested in the larger group of disciples around Jesus than in the Twelve. This larger group included women. At the end of the gospel, Mark reveals that these women had traveled with Jesus from Galilee to Jerusalem, heard the teachings, and seen the miracles. At the foot of the cross were "Mary Magdalene, and Mary the mother of James the younger and of Joses, and Salome. These used to follow him and provided for him when he was in Galilee; and there were many other women who had come up with him to Jerusalem" (15:40-41). As frequently noted, "followed" and "ministered" are important words for Mark. "Follow" is the technical term for discipleship in Mark. "Ministered" can be translated "served"; its root is the same as "deacon." It suggests, among other things, financial help, as Luke makes explicit in his account of Jesus' ministry, reporting that the woman "provided for Jesus [or "the disciples" or "Him" or "them" depending on the textual tradition followed] *out of their means* (8:3, italics mine). Apparently the women disciples both *had* some means of income over which they exerted control and used it to shoulder the financial burden of Jesus' ministry. Jeremias says, "the women among Jesus' followers . . . put their financial resources at his disposal."[41] They also probably put their reputations "on the line" by traveling with an itinerant male teacher and his male disciples and certainly put their own financial security in jeopardy by their generosity and their "following." They are true disciples.

The spectrum of the economic environment of Roman Palestine is clearly evident in Mark's narrative. We encounter small-business owners like James and John; the skilled craftsman, Jesus; tenant farming (12:1-12); and slavery which Jesus takes as a matter of course in 13:34, and, quite shockingly, uses as a metaphor for discipleship (10:44). One seldom sees modern scholars remarking on Jesus' apparent acceptance of slavery, which is odd since it goes against the grain of so much that he says about God's reign. It is an indication, I think, of how firmly entrenched a practice slavery was and reflects the cultural limitations of the evangelists. Mark's "economic picture" also includes the state of poverty and disease in which people lived and which so moved the heart of Jesus.

The economic oppression of Rome is evident in the person of Levi the tax collector (2:13) and in the important pericope in 12:13-17 as the Pharisees came to ask Jesus if taxes should be paid to Rome. They know, of course, that nonpayment of Roman taxes is an act of sedition. Scholars have held three views about this encounter. First, that Jesus was uninterested in matters of state since the Kingdom of God ends earthly kingdoms. Second, an "anti-Zealot view" holds Jesus refused to pay the tax but that this pericope offers no teaching on the state. Third, that payment of the tax suggests the state has "legitimate but provisional authority."[42] I wonder how greatly Mark's redaction, especially Jesus' words in 12:17, was influenced by the circumstances of his persecuted, Roman church. If the provenance of the gospel is Rome, this seems to me a particularly inflammatory story. Finally, we learn of the unjust treatment of widows, that most vulnerable class in society, by *religious* authorities, who would actively devour (*katesthiontes* suggests eating like an animal, thus "preying upon") widows' houses or passively accept in alms their "whole living" (12:38-44).

As the pairing of the religious officials and the widow indicates, Mark skillfully compares abundance and poverty and attitudes toward wealth by his placement of stories in the narrative. Another example is the picture of luxury and extravagance painted by Mark in the story of Herod's feast in 6:14-29 (which both Matthew and Luke compress) which is sharply contrasted with the hand-to-mouth life which necessitates the feeding of the five thousand in Galilee which immediately follows in 6:30-44. This pairing clarifies who the real king is: he of the Messianic Banquet, not the puppet king of Rome with his sleazy stag party (6:21). Mark's Jesus commends the abundance economics of God's reign, not those of Caesar and his appointees. In such pairing of opposites, Mark reveals his "Kingdom economics."

Mark's Kingdom Economics

If Mark's gospel addresses economic righteousness, and I indicated at the outset of the chapter wariness about how explicitly it does, it is in terms of distribution of wealth. In Mark there are those who hoard wealth and those who depend upon God's provision; those who take from others and those who give with liberality. For Mark, as for Jesus, "ethics are primarily *descriptive*; they illustrate how men and women behave in the kingdom."[43] Pairs of stories that exemplify these ethical contrasts and highlight Mark's economics are the rich man (10:17-31) with the widow's mite (12:38-44) and the plot against Jesus with the anointing woman (14:1-11). It is to them that we now turn.

We have already considered the story in 10:17-31 of the rich man whom Jesus loves for his adherence to the law; this man is the only person about whom this is said in Mark[44] (10:21). He is unable to divest himself of his possessions in order to "follow," to become a full disciple of Jesus (10:22). At his departure Jesus speaks of the general difficulty the rich have in entering the Kingdom and concludes that it is hard for everyone and only "possible with God" (10:27). If the rich man is the negative example in Mark's Kingdom economics, the poor widow of Jerusalem is the positive. She appears in direct contrast with the scribes "who devour widows' houses" (12:38).

The setting of her story is the Temple precincts where Jesus is teaching, which in Mark's view may well be "enemy territory," since, as noted, in a great Markan irony, the Temple is not the locus of holiness but a symbol of opposition to Jesus.[45] He denounces scribes for their egotism and avarice (12:39-40) and watches the rich contribute large sums of money, which they can well afford to do and which Jesus does not condemn (12:41). He sees a poor widow contribute two *lepta*, that tiniest coin, her "whole life" as the Greek so dramatically puts it (12:41-44). This widow's actions "prefigure those of Jesus, himself, who will shortly give his life as a ransom for many (see Mark 10:45)."[46] Did her action confirm for Jesus his own immediate future? Was her action prophetic as that of the anointing woman at Bethany in 14:3-9 so clearly was?

What Mark wants us to understand theologically, Mark tells us by the arrangement of stories in the narrative. In 12:38-44, I wonder if the primary message is the generosity of the widow (as the text is often preached) or the evil of a religious system which allows the most vulnerable members of the community feel they are economically responsible for it.[47] The point for Kingdom economics, however, is that of the astonishing generosity of the widow. She holds nothing back, gives all she has. The rich man could not follow Jesus because he had many possessions and could not give them up. She who had so little gives it all, as Jesus himself will do very shortly. In a section on "The Poor" in *Jesus Our Brother: The Humanity of the Lord*, Wilfrid Harrington notes that the rich "will find it very difficult to adapt to the world of the kingdom where everything will be shared. The rich will find it very painful to share."[48]

Another striking example of the plentitude of Kingdom economics appears at the outset of the Passion Narrative in chapter

14. It is an inclusion in which the account of the anointing woman (14:3-9) is sandwiched between the plot by Judas to betray Jesus (14:1-2 and 10-11). At Passover, a time both of solemn religious observance and of great political ferment since the root story of Passover is a story of liberation from oppression, the chief priests and scribes plot how to arrest Jesus "by stealth" (14:1). The picture Jesus has painted by word and deed of the superabundance of the Kingdom of God, its inclusiveness and generosity and grace, had great popular appeal. The religious authorities don't like it. When Judas Iscariot, one of the Twelve (another "religious insider") comes to them, they promise him money to betray Jesus (14:11).

While this plot is hatching, Jesus is just outside Jerusalem in Bethany feasting at the house of a leper. (We will revisit this story in the next chapter.) In this unlikely and improper company, a woman enters with a flask of extraordinarily expensive perfume and empties the whole thing on Jesus' head (14:13). What a waste! Three hundred denarii! The dinner guests do not understand Kingdom economics, but the woman does. Hers is the superabundance of Jesus' feeding miracles. The evangelist's is a Christological point which assumes we know that in Israel kings and prophets and priests and dead people were anointed. In terms of Mark's narrative, the woman's extravagant act of anointing is a sign act (perhaps like that of the generous widow), a prophecy indicating exactly what will follow. She seems to know Jesus is going to his death, that she has this last chance for an act of extravagant, loving service. If disciples are those who serve, she is a grand disciple! Jesus understands her act, "she has anointed my body beforehand for its burial" (14:8) and commends her so that "wherever the good news is proclaimed in the whole world, what she has done [is] will be told in remembrance of her" (14:9). By placing the betrayal of Judas and the anointing woman together, Mark contrasts venality and generosity, taking and giving. In Mark's maverick gospel it is not clean or unclean, religion or gender or race, "insider or outsider" status, but response to Jesus which is important.

For the evangelist, it is generosity and abundance, love of God manifested in care for neighbor that characterizes the economics of the Kingdom of God. And this fact suggests something else as well, which Thomas Green has noted. Jesus' "reacting to the criticism of the woman who anointed his head with costly ointment, which by implication was a criticism of himself for allowing her to do it, is scarcely the reaction of one for whom material poverty is of the very essence of the kingdom."[49] Nor, I would add, is it essential to one who promises homes, family and property, ironically, to those who leave all for his sake and the gospel. (See 10:29-30.) The attitude of Mark's Jesus toward possessions and wealth is a nuanced one. Wealth and possessions are not, of themselves, either good or bad. As Green suggests, "It is not what we possess but what we are attached to . . . which makes us unfit for, incapable of inheriting the kingdom of God."[50]

Conclusion

Hoppe asserts, "When the New Testament speaks of 'the poor,' it speaks both of the 'working poor' and the genuinely destitute. Members of both groups had little social status and no political power in the Roman world. They existed on the margins of society and were vulnerable to exploitation at the hands of the wealthy, both Jewish and Roman. The New Testament does not idealize poverty."[51] Indeed, "the term 'poor' always carries with it a sense of the experience of oppression and helplessness."[52] As Harrington pointedly and accurately asserts, "the 'poor' are not only those with few or no possessions, and not only those whose poverty is 'spiritual.' " In the biblical context the poor are the 'little people' who are incapable of standing up for themselves and hence, by reason of their need and sorry state, are God's protected ones."[53] "The emphasis is on the needy person, the one in distress. What is at stake. . .is one's attitude toward the little ones, the humble and the needy. The criterion is not the standard of religion or cult. . . . It is compassion."[54]

These oppressed and helpless "little ones" were the people Jesus took as his own. These were the people who loved him, and he gave them a vision that the way things are is not the way they were meant to be or, indeed, had to be. The great prophets of Israel had done no less. Echoing the prophets, Jesus' Kingdom economics held his tradition to its own highest standards. (See, for example, Exod 22:22-27; Deut 10:17-19 and 24:17-22.) The Law commanded care for the most vulnerable, and Hebrew Scripture taught that "the giving of alms was . . . a very important righteous work in the eyes of God."[55] The Markan Jesus called his own tradition to live up to its ideals. It is well past time for serious Christians in the Church to "follow" their Lord and do the same thing.

At a 2005 meeting of the Catholic Biblical Association of America, I heard a wonderful lecture by Professor Catherine Murphy titled "The Alternative Economy Envisioned in the Love Command."[56] Dr. Murphy pointed out that all three synoptic gospels record the double commandment to love God and neighbor (Mark 12:28-34; Matt 22:34-40; Luke 10:25-37) and asserted that commandment is the basis of God's alternative economy. L. D. Hurst concurs, noting that "this double command stands at the head of Jesus' ethical teaching as its quintessence."[57]

In the teaching of Jesus, love of God is manifested by love of neighbor, and particularly the needy neighbor. It is mercy and generosity like God's that the rich man lacks in all the synoptic accounts of him. "Indeed, one way for the wealthy to give tangible sign of their repentance is for them to distribute their goods to people in need."[58] Wealth is not itself evil; it can be used to do great good. "In dealing with wealth, Jesus does not suggest that wealth is evil in itself. . . . Wealth is a misfortune when . . . it distracts the rich from concern for the poor. It also tends to foster in the rich a feeling of security incompatible with that trust which God claims for himself alone. The admonition 'where your treasure is, there your heart will be also' (Luke 12:34) puts the matter in a nutshell."[59] Wealth can be used for good, but it also "seductively draws people away from total allegiance to God."[60]

The people we meet in the pages of Mark's gospel were all ruled by Empire. They were economically subject to another nation via taxation and to their own religious taxes. The command to love God and neighbor in the Torah, or on the lips of Jesus, is counter to Empire and the economics of Empire in which wealth is power. "Suffering and service, not nationalism and pride" was to constitute Christian life, "a role Jesus acted out in his own experience and which he encouraged in his friends."[61] To love God with all one's strength is to love God with one's material resources, to love like the widow with her two *lepta* and like the woman with her flask of expensive perfume. Jesus invited his disciples to constitute a new community in which those who might be enemies (tax collectors and Zealots, for example) became siblings, and those who had more than enough provided for those who had nothing. As Davids notes, "the call of Jesus to radical generosity is at one level an individual decision, but its context is that of a call to community."[62] "The kingdom of heaven is not, for the Jewish Jesus of Nazareth, a piece of real estate for the single saved soul; it is a communal vision of what could be and what should be. It is a vision of a time when all debts are forgiven, when we stop judging others, when we not only wear our traditions on our sleeve, but also hold them in our hearts and minds and enact them with all our strength."[63]

As Luke depicts the growth of the early church, it was at least in part this compassionate community that attracted new disciples. "All who believed were together and had all things in common; they would sell their possessions and goods and distribute the proceeds to all, as any had need"; "And day by day the Lord added to their number" (Acts 2:44-45, 47). "[N]o one claimed private ownership of any possessions, but everything they owned was held in common"; "There was not a needy person among them, for as many as owned lands or houses sold them and brought the proceeds of what was sold" (Acts 4:32, 34).[64]

To love with money, which symbolizes strength or might or personal autonomy, is to align oneself with Jesus' new community and with God's Kingdom economics. To hoard it is to remain firmly in the kingdoms of this world with their evil schemes of scarcity. Worldly economics operates by valuing what is scarce (which is why diamonds are expensive and potatoes aren't) and thus gives the message that there is not enough to go around. And so like Jesus' beloved rich man, people hoard and go away sad. But the economics of the Kingdom of God is an economics of abundance. "Jesus consistently pictured the consummation of the kingdom as a time of plenty."[65] John Koenig puts the point very clearly: "If there is one single metaphor for the kingdom that stands out from all the others, it is that of God's abundance, graciously offered to all in festive meals."[66]

Mark's Kingdom economics suggest that there is more than enough to go around when we share what is, in any case, God's. This is the point of the two feeding stories of the Markan Jesus and of his response to the Pharisees on taxation: render "to God the things that are God's." What *isn't* God's? Mark's Kingdom economics and the economy of the Kingdom of God are about giving to receive and of having more when you finish giving than you had when you started. The kingdoms of this world and their rulers and many of their citizens have never "gotten it." But the biblical promise of Mark's untamed gospel is that one day the kingdoms of this world will become the Kingdom of our Lord, and of his Christ. And then, Mark might ask, who will be holding the purse strings?

Chapter 4

Brother Jesus: Asceticism and Its Implications in Mark[1]

Thus far in our consideration of Mark's "untamed" gospel, we have examined his focus on suffering, the general subject of discipleship, and the more specific subject of "Kingdom economics." This chapter may present the biggest challenge and perhaps the biggest reward since looking at familiar material from a new or slightly different perspective can give fresh insights about what we think we know well. I do not set out to prove that St. Mark was a proto-Benedictine. I will not even argue that Mark knowingly wrote from the perspective of asceticism, although that religious impulse clearly existed in the first century. I hope to highlight some major themes in Mark's gospel that resonate with a trajectory common to most world religions and brought into focus for Christians in the life and teaching of Jesus summarized by the phrase *basilea tou theou* (kingdom or reign of God) which occurs fourteen times in this gospel.[2]

First, I will review the linguistic field and some examples of asceticism in the New Testament period. Second, I will introduce two modern formulations of asceticism: (a) that it is primarily personal religious practice, and (b) that it is primarily an attitude toward dominant culture (although from that attitude, certain practices may arise). We shall examine how Mark's gospel does and doesn't fit these two templates. Finally, I gently suggest that images of asceticism in Mark's gospel highlight the *basilea tou theou*, "the heart of Jesus' teaching," "a universal, spiritual order in which humankind could find the fulfillment of its ultimate desires for righteousness, justice, peace . . . and a restored relationship to God."[3] The *basilea tou theou* is shorthand for the new "way" Jesus preaches and inaugurates. Asceticism in Mark's gospel is closely aligned with discipleship, the *basilea tou theou* which Dennis Dulling calls an " 'ethic' which reverses accepted social norms"[4] and the community it envisions in contradistinction to the ruling order, be it Jewish or Greco-Roman. In Mark's maverick gospel, asceticism is about discipleship and the *basilea*.

Interestingly, a significant body of material exists not only on asceticism in the Greco-Roman period, represented in the work of Richard Valantasis and Vincent L. Wimbush[5], but also asceticism in the New Testament. Chapter 4 of von Campenhausen's *Tradition and Life in the Church: Essays and Lectures on Church History* (1968) is an extended study of early Christian asceticism.[6] J. Duncan Derrett has written a book on the Sermon on the Mount as "ascetic discourse."[7] Major studies by Wimbush and John S. Kloppenborg, Robert Murray, Stephen J. Patterson, Anthony L. Saldarini, Mary Ann Tolbert, and Leif E. Vaage examine various aspects of the phenomenon.[8]

Linguistic Field and Historical Precedents

The root of the English word "asceticism" is the Greek verb *askeo* (to practice, to train, to engage in some activity) and the derivative *askesis* (exercise, practice, and training). It is most commonly found in Greco-Roman writing in the context of training athletes, although, in general, *asketes* connoted one who practiced a particular art, trade, or lifestyle.[9] *Askeo* occurs in the New Testament only in Acts 24:16 where, in Caesarea, Paul tells Felix that he "exercises" or "exerts" himself to have a clear conscience toward God and people. Although he uses a related word, it seems odd that Paul does not use the term in 1 Corinthians 9:25ff when he describes his self-discipline, especially in view of the fact that the term is "so common in Jewish Hellenism and later Christian literature."[10] Vaage correctly notes that *askeo* originally meant "training," not specific renunciations.[11] "The term is used by Homer for artistic endeavor but is then applied spiritually from Herodotus and Pindar and occurs in the Stoics for taming the passions, exercise in virtue, and thought control. Philo finds in Jacob the model *asketes* on the basis of Gen. 32.34f."[12] Greek and Roman philosophers used the term in the context of moral training, for voluntary abstention, for practices carried out to combat vice and develop virtue, and from this developed the common connotation of asceticism as the renunciation of customary comforts for religious purposes.[13]

Askesis was related to *enkrateia* with the root *krat*, "denoting power or lordship." Thus *enkrates* means "having power over all things and the self." Socrates, Aristotle, and the Stoics used the term for the moral virtue of self-restraint. It is valued in Philo, by the Essenes, and in the Hermetic writings as well as in the LXX. Although not occurring in the gospels, Paul uses it in 1 Corinthians 7:9 for sexual self-control and 9:25 for athletic self-control.[14] Kallistos Ware noted that in Greco-Roman antiquity *anachoresis* and *enkrateia* were pathways to joy and happiness, and he argues persuasively that the basic impulse behind *enkrateia* in Christian teaching is positive moderation.[15] Following Ware, Stephen Patterson points out that in the early Jesus tradition *enkrateia* represented not "war with flesh" but reducing "life to its simplest form . . . to reaffirm creation's basic goodness and adequacy."[16] This is worth keeping in mind. Asceticism is not viewed as life-denying but as training in enjoying what is enough, a point surely related to Mark's "Kingdom economics," and training from which our culture would certainly benefit.

The final term in the lexical field of asceticism in the New Testament is the aforementioned *anachoreo*, the verb meaning "to withdraw, to go away, to retire," and, oddly enough, in some instances "to return." It is found in parallel literature with the meaning of "absence," and it has been argued that both "to flee" and "to take refuge" are good translations, the latter, according to Moulton and Milligan, suiting "most of the NT passages remarkably well."[17] Although used more frequently by Matthew, Mark uses *anachoreo* in 3:7 to describe Jesus' withdrawal after his Sabbath healing of a man with a withered hand and subsequent confrontation with the odd alliance of customary enemies, Pharisee and Herodians (3:1-6). Linking *anachoreo* with Jesus' three private prayer periods in Mark (1:35; 6:45-46; 14:32-35), Mary Ann Tolbert remarks that "the presence of the world continues with Jesus" in 3:7-8. Jesus carries the world with him when he withdraws.[18] Indeed, I would argue that Jesus withdraws so that he *can* return. We will return to the concept of "withdrawal" shortly. For the moment, note that Mark's gospel is drawn not only into the lexical field of asceticism, but into one of its characteristic practices and attitudes.

Although perhaps not extensively, the vocabulary of asceticism in the Greco-Roman world appears in the New Testament. That the ascetic impulse was common in the philosophical and religious environment of early Christianity is well documented, and in spite of the Reformers' attempt to whitewash the fact, early Christianity itself was often viewed as essentially ascetic. Indeed, integrating the asceticism of Gnostics, Manicheans, the Encratites, Messalians, and other groups was focal in early struggles toward what became Christian orthodoxy. How monasticism in the fourth century resolved the problem is another study for another time. As Columba Stewart noted in his essay, "Christian Spirituality during the Roman Empire (100–600)," asceticism "was a current in Christian practice from earliest times, reflecting the ascetical orientation of some Jewish groups."[19]

James Goehring says simply, "The ascetic ideal . . . was part of most early Christian theology."[20] Furthermore, he thinks that Jewish asceticism had its roots in the Holiness Codes and restrictions designed to define covenantal relationship. Observant Jews were to be holy because their God was holy (Lev 11:44). Holy behavior is frequently in contradistinction to that commonly practiced in the dominant culture. I need hardly give examples. In any case, the idea of self-mastery undergirded the ethical teaching of Greco-Roman philosophers and much teaching in the Wisdom books of the LXX. Josephus' teacher Bannus (*Vit* 2), Philo's fascinating description of the Therapeuta in Egypt (*Contemplative Life*), the Essenes (whom Fr. Murray believes were the dominant influence on the development of Christian asceticism[21]), and the figure of John the Baptist all attest to Jewish asceticism in our period and in Mark's environment.[22]

Similarly, Plato's cosmological dualism (simply put, if this world is but a shadow, not the Reality, it is best to be detached from it) supplied the philosophical base for Greco-Roman aestheticism which is well documented in Vincent L. Wimbush's *Ascetic Behavior in Greco-Roman Antiquity: A Sourcebook*.[23] Certainly withdrawal (*anachoresis*) into the self was a fundamental tenant of Stoicism, perhaps the most influential philosophical movement of the New Testament period.[24] Although it is hard to make a case that the "glutton and drunkard" Jesus (Matt 11:19) was himself an ascetic, those who were called to discipleship, and who began to imitate the self-sacrificial life of Jesus very quickly began to manifest features of what we now call asceticism. (Paradoxically, however, self-emptying, *kenosis*, does not mean rejection of moderate use and enjoyment of the good things of the world and the senses.) We see the process of aspects of discipleship moving toward asceticism in Mark's gospel.

Definitions of Asceticism as Templates for Analyzing Mark's Gospel

In doing background reading on asceticism, I noted that the modern scholarly definitions of the phenomenon tend to follow one of two trajectories. Either they define asceticism in terms of practices (fasting, celibacy, etc.) undertaken for a religious end or they understand it as an attitude toward the dominant culture. The following are examples of the first or "practice" type of definition:

- "a voluntary, sustained, and at least partially systematic program of self-discipline and self-denial in which immediate, sensual, or profane gratifications are renounced in order to attain a higher spiritual state or a more thorough absorption in the sacred" (Walter Kaelber, *Encyclopedia of Religion*).[25]
- "any act of self-denial undertaken as a strategy of empowerment or gratification" (Geoffrey Harpham, *The Ascetic Imperative in Culture and Criticism*).[26]

- "voluntary exercise of self-denial designed to separate the individual from the human world and thereby facilitate access to the divine" (*Encyclopedia of Early Christianity*).[27]
- renouncing aspects of customary social life and comfort or adopting painful conditions for religious purposes (*The Oxford Dictionary of the Christian Church*).[28]
- "sustained practice of physical and spiritual disciplines" (Columba Stewart).[29]

In the "practice" category of definition, asceticism is defined in terms of "things done and left undone." The "attitude" category defines asceticism in terms of one's critical stance vis-à-vis dominant culture. Here are some examples:

- The driving force of asceticism is "a renunciation of success in the world" (Henry Chadwick).[30]
- "The ascetic is one who makes a conscious decision to lay down the script, to step outside of conventional roles, outside of the familiar world of commonly assumed values, activities, plans, agendas" (Stephen Patterson).[31]
- "asceticism begins to operate when an alternative to the social and religious givens developed." The intention is "to inaugurate a new subjectivity, different social relations, and an alternative symbolic universe" (Richard Valantasis).[32]

In this second category of definition the focus is on the motivation for whatever practices might be undertaken. That motivation is clearly dissatisfaction with dominant culture, a sense that "the way things are" either is not what they should be, or is an active impediment to religious knowledge, spiritual progress, holiness, or all three. That the *basilea* of Caesar (or Temple or church) is not the *basilea tou theou* requires an active response. These two trajectories of definition provide useful templates for examining asceticism in Mark's gospel to which we now turn.

Mark's Gospel and the Practice of Asceticism

One modern understanding of Christian asceticism (which I find highly influenced by monasticism's later development) is that it is consciously chosen practices or actions consciously rejected for religious or spiritual reasons. Such an understanding points toward one of Mark's major themes, one treated in some detail in chapter 2—discipleship. Markan scholars generally agree that one of the evangelist's primary concerns is what it means to be a disciple of Jesus. Most suggest that the central section and spatial center of the gospel, 8:22-10:52, focuses on discipleship, and in this section six of Mark's fourteen uses of "kingdom of God" occur.[33] The idea is expressed succinctly by Ernest Best in *Disciples and Discipleship*: "The rule of discipleship is: Jesus. As Jesus was, so the disciple must be."[34] "Follow" (*akolutheo*) is the invitation to discipleship in Mark. As von Campenhausen notes, "come follow me" is an invitation to do what the Master does.[35] What the Master does, he concludes, is to exhibit an early Christian asceticism.

Von Campenhausen argues that Jesus literally meant his followers to sell and give away all their possessions. "The sacrifice of home, family, possessions resulted . . . from the way of life which Jesus, homeless and poor, called his disciples to share."[36] Unconditional personal adhesion to the Lord, accepted in faith, resulted in openness to every concrete form of demand, and in particular, abandoning property, abstinence from food, and renunciation of marriage and sexuality. Von Campenhausen calls these three practices the signs of asceticism in relation to early Christian teaching and the "special form and implementation of the 'following' of Jesus."[37] It will be clarifying briefly to explore the degree to which Mark's gospel reflects renunciation of property, dietary abstinence, and sexual abstinence expressed as retreat from marriage and family. In Mark's narrative and environment, each to some degree represents radicality we might well term "maverick."

Renunciation of Property

From the outset of the gospel, the call of Simon and Andrew who left their nets and of James and Zebedee who abandoned boat, father, and servants (1:16-20), Jesus' teaching and example is wary of the accumulation of possessions. His disciples "leave things behind" when they follow him. When he sends the Twelve out to teach, "He ordered them to take nothing for their journey except a staff; no bread, no bag, no money in their belts; but to wear sandals and not to put on two tunics" (6:8-9). As noted in the previous chapter, perhaps the most dramatic example of renunciation of possessions occurs when Jesus encounters the rich man who has observed the law. Mark tells us that Jesus "loved him," but commands "go, sell what you own, and give the money to the poor . . . and come, follow me" (10:20-21). This rich man cannot do.

Interestingly, the Markan theme of women as exemplary disciples (at least until the last scene of the gospel) is consistent with the invitation (for it is never a demand) to ascetic renunciation of property. Although, like other scholars, I tend to read the story of the "widow's mite" (12:41-44) in the context of Jesus' criticism of the scribes[38] (12:38-40), in contrast to the rich man, the poor widow does give away all she has, "her whole living" (literally, "her whole life," 12:44). Similarly, disregarding the cost of the ointment ("more than 300 denarii," 14:5), the anointing woman in 14:3-9 seems more concerned with Jesus' well-being and her devotion to him than to preserving her wealth. It is striking that immediately after we see her generosity, Mark shows Judas "selling Jesus out" for money (14:10-11).

Although perhaps not with the focused clarity of the Lukan writings, Mark's gospel reflects asceticism with regard to property. Asceticism with regard to food and drink is less evident.

Dietary Abstinence

Von Campenhausen comments that, with regard to abstinence from food and drink, it is "abundantly clear how little Christianity was, originally, an ascetical movement."[39] Mark's gospel bears this out. Mark's Jesus appears regularly at, and indeed, hosts dinners and feasts (2:15-17; 6:30-44; 8:1-10; 14:3; 14:12-15). In Mark 2:18-20 the disciples of John the Baptist and the Pharisees are scandalized that Jesus' disciples do not fast. The only reason Mark supplies for why Jesus' disciples miss meals is overwork: "the crowd came together again, so that they could not even eat" (3:20) and "many were coming and going, and they had no leisure even to eat" (6:31). How Jesus' disciples eat (washed or unwashed) seems of more interest to the Pharisees and scribes in 7:1-8 than whether they eat. Apparently they do eat, or the question of washing wouldn't have arisen. In the Jewish context, the Markan Jesus apparently declares "all foods clean" (7:19), although there is lively scholarly debate about what this meant. (And see chap. 2, note 31.)

I suggested earlier that the miracle in Mark's two feeding stories (the five thousand in 6:30-44 and the four thousand in 8:1-10) is precisely the leftovers, the abundance—twelve baskets and seven baskets of leftovers respectively. We will return to this point later. For now note that Mark includes two feeding stories: one in Jewish territory (chap. 6) and, after Jesus' encounter with the Syrophoenician woman in chapter 7, one in Gentile territory (chap. 8)—both as part of his general interest in a Gentile ministry and to indicate the inclusiveness of God's abundance.

There is another approach to dietary abstinence that is quite interesting. In a discussion of Jesus' table fellowship J. D. G. Dunn points out that whom one ate with (or declined to eat with) was a way of keeping pure and of professing Israel's separateness.[40] Mark's Jesus exhibits concern for purity of motivation or intention more than for practice, and this is consistent with the evangelist's interest in the Gentile mission. On the other hand, the Pharisees and their disciples fast, thus observing boundary maintenance (Mark 2:18). Following Bruce Malina's 1986 work on Christian origins and cultural anthropology, Neufeld's study of Jesus' "eating habits" points out that "fasting is a ritualized behavior that has both a vertical dimension, directed to God, and a horizontal one, directed to members within one's group."[41] Fasting not only "communicates with God" but serves to maintain boundaries within a group and symbolizes group affiliation. "That Jesus and his disciples reject the practice of fasting indicates that they had no concern about upholding existing boundaries."[42] And Jesus has already eaten in the house of a tax collector and with "sinners" (2:15-18) and will dine in the house of Simon the Leper (14:3), thus having broken boundaries fasting helped to maintain.

In any case, I do not see much evidence of asceticism with regard to food and drink in Mark's gospel. But it is important to bear in mind that there is a certain luxury connected with fasting. Only those who aren't starving have the luxury of fasting. Fasting was an enormous physical burden in a subsistence culture like the one described in the previous chapter, and the fact that Jews engaged in it to express mourning or to influence God in favor of their petitions is noteworthy. Indeed, Mark's Jesus feeds the multitudes precisely in compassion for their hunger: "I have compassion for the crowd, because they have been with me now three days and have nothing to eat. If I send them away hungry to their homes, they will faint on the way—and some of them have come from a great distance" (8:2-3). For Mark's Jesus, charity trumps whatever asceticism might be operative.

Sexual Abstinence and Family Life

If Mark's gospel exhibits asceticism with regard to possessions but not with regard to food and drink, the picture with regard to sexual abstinence and family life is mixed. Von Campenhausen notes that Jewish piety "was not in the least ascetically inclined as regards sexual matters."[43] As Osiek and Balch have so clearly demonstrated in *Families in the New Testament World: Households and House Churches*, family was the dominant social institution in the period, providing identity, nurture, education, and physical security.[44] To reject family was not only distinctly odd, but personally dangerous and potentially a challenge to the social order.

Mark's Jesus delivers no explicit prohibition against sex or marriage. Mark's gospel bears out von Campenhausen's dictum that "asceticism in the sexual sphere plays no part . . . in the older stratum of revelation common to all the evangelists."[45] Certainly Br. Jesus does not hesitate to associate with, or perform miracles for, women, nor does he recoil from the extravagant and sensual service rendered by the anointing woman whose action he defends (14:3-9). In 10:5-12 when the Pharisees come to test Jesus with a question about divorce, his response is very pro-marriage. But in a similar conflict story when the Sadducees come with their tale of the poor woman who was passed around in a family of seven brothers (12:18-27), Jesus says that when people "rise from the dead, they neither marry nor are given in marriage, but are like angels in heaven" (12:25). Does Jesus mean the unmarried state is more heavenly, more like the angels? Is that because in his religious community "unmarried" meant "celibate" or "chaste"?

The forerunner, John the Baptist, was apparently unmarried, as, apparently, was Jesus, and "the disciples, in following him, cut themselves off from their families and relatives."[46] Again, the Markan Jesus exhibits a variety of attitudes toward marriage, the acceptable context for sexual activity in Judaism. In 1:16-20 he seems not to worry that the fishermen he calls to follow him leave behind family and what were culturally very strong family ties and important responsibilities. Later in the gospel the issue reappears after the rich man who can't sell all leaves, and Peter says, "Look, we have left everything and followed you" (10:28). Everything means everything: "house or brothers or sisters or mother or father or children or fields" (10:29). "Lands," as we learned in the previous chapter, meant "wealth" and is a metaphor for wealth. Jesus promises his disciples a hundredfold compensation and "in the age to come eternal life" (10:30). Mark does not record Peter's reaction to this promise with its intimated social reorganization: "many who are first will be last, and the last will be first" (10:31).

Jesus' declaration that an itinerant preaching ministry "is what I came out to do" (1:38) implicitly rejects his own family responsibilities which is particularly odd if, as tradition suggests, he is the oldest son and leaves behind a widowed mother. (John solves this problem in his gospel at 19:25-27 when the dying Jesus entrusts his mother to the beloved disciple.) Little wonder that Jesus' biological family thought popular opinion that "He has gone out of his mind" (3:21) or is possessed by Beelzebul (3:22) might be accurate. When Jesus' mother and brothers come to him, his response is, at first, enigmatic: "Who are my mother and my brothers?" (3:33). Jesus uses this as an occasion radically to redefine family from being a matter of blood kinship to being a matter of discipleship. "Whoever does the will of God is my brother and sister and mother" (3:35). The definition clearly includes his mother who, by it, is the *first* disciple. John Painter rightly describes this redefinition as "a critique which precludes tribalism in favour of a relationship appropriate to a universal movement."[47]

While Jesus sends the healed Gerasene Demoniac home to preach to family and friends (5:19) and upholds the commandments with regard to honoring parents (7:10-13), in the apocalyptic discourse in chapter 13 he also warns of disruption within the biological family: "Brother will betray brother to death, and a father his child, and children will rise against parents and have them put to death" (13:12). (So much for the exemplary biblical family!) Perhaps this warning reflects Jesus' own bitter experience of being rejected in Nazareth (6:1-6). Jesus does not explicitly condemn sexual intercourse, although so far as we know he was celibate, nor does he condemn marriage, although his attitude toward family in Mark's gospel is ambiguous.

Leif E. Vaage gives us an interesting and valuable alternative reading of the evidence in his article, "An Other Home: Discipleship in Mark as Domestic Asceticism." He defines asceticism according to our second trajectory as "to live 'against the grain' of whatever is taken to be . . . normative in a given cultural context, in order to experience here and now . . . a better or 'larger' life."[48] Vaage argues that the household is where this is practiced because discipleship unfolds in the domestic setting: Capernaum, Levi's home, the "house of Simon the leper."[49] He terms discipleship in Mark "an alternative domesticity," a "contrary" and "subversive" social state, a "Place of deep withdrawal from prevailing social practices," from which the follower first withdraws from the world in order to save his life there.[50]

Withdrawal

While basically understanding asceticism as attitude, Vaage's reading of family and household in Mark highlights one more traditional ascetic practice that seems characteristic of the Markan Jesus—withdrawal (*anachoreo*). As previously noted, Mark uses the term at 3:7 when, after the confrontation with the Pharisees and Herodians, "And Jesus with his disciples withdrew (*anachoresen*) to the sea" (my translation). To "withdraw," especially during his intense public ministry, is a characteristic action of the Markan Jesus, evident in 1:12-13 (the wilderness temptation where, in fact, he is driven out into the wilderness); 1:35-36 (he goes to a deserted place to pray); 3:13ff (on the mountain); 6:30ff (invites disciples to a deserted place); 6:45-46 (sends disciples away and withdraws to pray); 7:24 (enters a house and doesn't want it known); 8:13 (withdraws alone in the boat?). In the final week in Jerusalem, Jesus withdraws from the city at night and returns to Bethany, and he withdraws to Gethsemani for the last agonizing and lonely prayer vigil (14:32ff.). Mark calls Jesus "teacher" more frequently than any other evangelist (and records the fewest of his words), and it has been noted that the Markan Jesus is a great healer. I would suggest he is also a great contemplative, if withdrawal from the world or at least from the spheres of public activity for prayer is any indication of a contemplative bent.

There was apparently something about "everyday life," perhaps the unexamined desire for possessions, food, family, something about "the way things were," in the conduct of ministry that necessitated Jesus' withdrawal. Perhaps in this, Mark's Jesus exemplifies a healthy balance clearly absent in modern work-obsessed culture. Goehring points out that "parents and property . . . bound one to the present age."[51] And if Mark 13 is any indication, the "present age" was in big trouble. It is exactly this dynamic that is expressed in the second understanding of asceticism: that it is primarily a critical attitude toward dominant culture.

Mark's Gospel and the Attitude of Asceticism

Asceticism with regard to possessions, food and drink, and family were undertaken to give the follower of Jesus freedom *from* constraints on full discipleship and freedom *for* the *basilea tou theou*, the new way of living Jesus envisioned and preached. Kallistos Ware believes that asceticism is for transfiguration not mortification of the body.[52] I would add that this transformation is both for the body personal and the body public. Asceticism includes the personal and individual as well as the public and communal. Ascetic practices are *ipso facto* individual; ascetical attitudes address (indeed, often challenge) public, communal life.

In a fascinating (if immensely dense) article entitled "Constructions of Power in Asceticism" (which has greatly influenced my thinking on this issue), Richard Valantasis argues that "asceticism begins to operate when an alternative to the social and religious givens is developed."[53] There are three formative aspects of the process: developing alternatives to the prescribed cultural subjectivity, restructuring social relations, and developing an alternative symbolic universe.[54] Ascetic practices like rejection of possessions, food or family are undertaken "precisely in order to embrace another existence," "another way of living embodied in a new subjectivity, alternative social relations, and a new imaging of the universe. And this intentionality has power . . . to create a new person . . . to restructure society . . . to revise the understanding of the universe."[55] In short, asceticism has social reorganization as one of its goals. Christian asceticism as we see it in Mark has as a goal social reorganization away from "what is" and toward the *basilea tou theou*. The point of Jesus' preaching is that the way things are isn't the way they are supposed to be and *can be changed.* As was what we called in the previous chapter the Markan Jesus' "Kingdom economics," this is a message of hope.

Stephen Patterson opens his article "Askesis and the Early Jesus Tradition" with the question, "What shall we make of someone who leaves house and home to pursue the life of a mendicant holy man, eschewing family, village, economic stability, and religious acceptance?"[56] I would respond, "We make of such a person one who perceives something askew, something slightly, or even greatly, wrong with the commonly accepted or dominant family, social, economic and religious systems." Such a person is an "attitudinal ascetic," one who renounces the customary because the customary has gone very seriously awry. Patterson concludes, "the ascetic is one who makes a conscious decision to lay down the script, to step outside of conventional roles, outside of the familiar world of commonly assumed values, activities, plans, agendas."[57]

Mark's Jesus is such an "attitudinal ascetic." He rejects customary and accepted patterns in favor of the new way of the *basilea tou theou*. And to invite others to follow him, to be disciples, is to invite them to accept this critical attitude and to assist in constructing his alternative vision. At the risk of imposing a modern schema on an ancient document, let me point out how the Markan Jesus exhibits Valantasis' three formative aspects.

Alternatives to the Prescribed Cultural Subjectivity

It isn't difficult to see where I am going with regard to Mark's gospel. Mark's Jesus often criticizes and sometimes renounces the established order of things. He is the sort of ascetic who envisions an alternative society in contradistinction to the existing one. One need only remember his apple-cart-upsetting teachings about power after the second and third passion predictions. "Whoever wants to be first, must be last of all and servant of all" (9:35). Then after James and John ask for the seats at Jesus' right and left in glory (10:37), the best seats (fifty-yard line or dress circle!) in heaven, Jesus describes the great reordering in the *basilea*. "You know that among the Gentiles those whom they recognize as their rulers lord it over them, and their great ones are tyrants over them. But it is not so among you [that is, among those making up the "alternative" community of disciples]; but whoever wishes to become great among you must be your servant, and whoever wishes to be first among you must be slave of all" (10:42-44). As David F. Watson asserts in a recent article, "the Gospel of Mark . . . reverses the system of values that define the qualities of the power elite."[58] And what is the precedent for such a shocking reversal? Jesus himself. "For the Son of Man came not to be served but to serve, and to give his life a ransom for many" (10:45). Such teaching was (and is) radical and dangerous.

What was Jesus' attitude toward the prevailing Jewish and Roman "cultural subjectivities"? As an example of the first we might, as J. D. G. Dunn does, take the notion of "purity." Purity and holiness, with which purity goes hand in hand, were major preoccupations of Judaism, definitive for Jewish identity. (See Lev 11:1-23; Deut 14:3-21.) Dunn explores whether or not Jesus undermined the purity code with regard to food, fellowship, and healing, and comes to a mixed conclusion.[59] Whatever we conclude must take into account an important question Dunn raises but doesn't answer definitively: if Jesus completely set aside purity, why was Peter so worried about it in Acts 10?[60] In Jewish Scripture and teaching, to be holy as God is holy is not primarily to be spiritually pious but to be just ("righteous" as per chap. 3), to exhibit in one's own actions the nature of the God of whom the prophets spoke.

As an example of Roman "cultural subjectivity" we might revisit the matter of taxation which was discussed in chapter 3 and helpfully clarified by John Donahue.[61] Tax collectors, he pointed out, were Jews who, in the popular mind, were at best engaged in dishonest occupations and, at worst, were quislings. Tax collectors in Galilee served under Herod Antipas but were no more acceptable for that. So, when Jesus calls Levi the son of Alphaeus to "follow," to become a disciple, and then dines with him and "many tax collectors and sinners" (2:13-17), he defies popular opinion and guidelines for appropriate table companions. Even the hated Roman taxes and those who collected them were not determinative of fellowship for Jesus whose table fellowship exhibited a radical inclusivity.

Taxes appear again significantly in one of the Jerusalem controversy stories when those unlikely allies, the Pharisees (who must have opposed Roman taxes) and Herodians (who were willing to live with them), raise the question, "Is it lawful to pay taxes to the emperor, or not?" (12:14). The issue for them was not paying taxes but "to trap [Jesus] in what he said" (12:13). For Jesus, however, taxes are apparently the symbol of "Caesar's kingdom." As noted in the previous chapter, the command, "Give to the emperor the things that are the emperor's, and to God the things that are God's" (12:17), has elicited at least three lines of interpretation: (1) Jesus is not interested in obligations to the state as God's kingdom ends earthly kingdoms; (2) Jesus indirectly refuses to pay the tax but gives no teaching on the state; (3) The "two reigns" interpretation suggests that the state has legitimate but provisional authority.[62] One's interpretation depends upon the reading of "the things of God" (*ta tou theou to theo*). The implicit question, of course, is "What *isn't* God's?" How ever one reads the passage, it is clear that taxes, the symbol of Roman domination, are not of great import to Jesus who, as an itinerant, didn't pay land tax or customs tax or transport tax on goods.

Restructuring Social Relations

The second of Valantasis' three formative aspects of asceticism is "restructuring of social relations," and this, too, is clearly evident in Mark's gospel. Two examples will suffice: the precedent-breaking inclusivity of Jesus' table fellowship to which we have alluded in the person of Levi, and his attitude toward and interactions with women which I have highlighted throughout this book.

The work of Bartchy, Corley, Malina, Neyrey, Rohrbaugh, and other scholars have provided extraordinarily important insights into the practices and meaning of table fellowship in the New Testament world.[63] An article by Dietmar Neufeld applies their work specifically to Mark's gospel. Neufeld notes that "Food marks social differences, boundaries, bonds, and contradictions."[64] Placing meals in the context of honor contests, he analyzes what he calls "Jesus' eating transgressions and social impropriety" in Mark, focusing particularly on Jesus dining with Levi (2:13-17), the dispute about plucking grain on the Sabbath (2:23-28), the problem of eating with defiled hands (7:1-23), the food metaphor in Jesus' encounter with the Syrophoenician woman (7:24-30) which he rightly notes is bracketed by feeding stories. Neufeld concludes that Jesus "disregards . . . distinctions and recklessly violates any sense of decorum through his choice of table companions." "Eating, food, and table fellowship mark the transformation of social relations." "Table fellowship . . . symbolizes the establishment of relationships based not so much on the conventions of social stratification as on a radically inclusive companionship in which boundaries between people are being broken down."[65] In short, Jesus "restructures social relationships" in his rejection of the exclusionary aspect of table fellowship as it was customarily practiced.

A similar pattern of rejection and reordering is evident in Jesus' attitude toward and fellowship with women in Mark. Although there are only five named women in Mark (Mary, the mother of Jesus; Herodias; Mary Magdalene; Mary the mother of James and Joses; Salome), roughly one-fourth of the characters in the gospel are women, perhaps more since the frequently used general terms "crowd" and "disciples" included women. Women are central in thirteen pericopae in the narrative (1:30-31; 3:31-35; 5:21-24, 35-43; 5:24-32; 6:3, 14-29; 7:24-30; 12:41-44; 14:3-9, 66-69; 15:40-41, 47; 16:1-8), most important, in Mark's resurrection account where, after having been model disciples throughout the narrative, they too fall short, exemplifying again Mark's point that discipleship is both gender inclusive and a process in which nobody is perfect.[66]

If I were to be so arrogant as to fault the evangelist Mark, which admiring his gospel (and, incidentally, believing it) I am not, I would criticize his placement of the most important bit of information about women in the gospel. Almost at the end of the narrative, at the foot of the cross, "There were. . .women looking on from a distance" (the two Marys and Salome), who "used to follow him and provided for him when he was in Galilee; and there were many other women who had come up with him to Jerusalem" (15:40-41). Mark indicates that from the outset of the Galilean ministry, women "followed," the technical term for discipleship. They "served" Jesus and, along with "many other women," came with Jesus from Galilee to Jerusalem. As Elizabeth Struthers Malbon has noted, in Mark, *akoloutheo* always denotes commitment of some kind and *diakoneo* is the essence of messianic ministry and discipleship.[67] We have to read this information back onto the whole narrative, especially the crucial discipleship section because it means that the group around Jesus included women who heard his teaching, saw his miracles, and are included in his commands.

More specifically, in three of five important scenes in which women are models of discipleship, Jesus breaches social convention and/or religious purity regulations: healing of Simon's mother-in-law (1:30-31), the woman with the flow of blood (5:24-34), and the encounter with the Syrophoenician woman (7:24-30). The latter two are particularly potent examples of including the excluded. Certainly no more dramatic example could be cited of Jesus' openness to women than Mark's account of the anointing woman whose action occurs in the boundary-breaking location of "the house of Simon the *leper*" (14:3, italics mine). Her gesture is not only extravagantly generous (like that of the widow in 12:41-44), and sensual, but prophetic of Jesus' impending death (14:3-9). And Jesus responds not by recoiling in horror but by commending her, and if not criticizing, at least chiding others at table with him. The Galilean rabbi publicly shames her critics by disagreeing with them in favor of a woman. This is volatile stuff.

Developing an Alternative Symbolic Universe

The third formative aspect of "attitudinal asceticism" as Valantasis defines it is the conscious development of an alternative symbolic universe. This, of course, is the whole point of a gospel: to narrate the beginning of the "alternative symbolic universe" first called "Christian" in Antioch (Acts 11:26). I may be guilty of finding what I am looking for, but it seems to me that Mark's unusual depiction of Jerusalem and the Temple is an indication that he intends to replace one set of symbols with another. I have argued elsewhere (and earlier in this book) that Mark views Jerusalem negatively as the source of opposition to Jesus, and that, in the Temple, the evangelist inherited an ambiguous symbol.[68] Although attitudes toward it varied, the Second Temple was the symbol of God's presence with the people of Israel, of Israel's cultic life, of the forgiveness of sins. But in Mark's narrative, Jerusalem represents opposition to Jesus, and the Temple at its center is largely depicted negatively. Jesus' last week opens with his cursing a fig tree (11:13-14), the first bracket of an inclusion which closes with 11:20-25 and surrounds Jesus' Temple cleansing (11:15-19). Sharyn Dowd and others read the fig tree as a symbol of the Temple's barrenness.[69] Jesus both attacks the Temple and defends its legitimacy as "a house of prayer for *all the nations*" (11:15-19, 17, italics mine). In part as a result of this attitude, Jesus engages in hostile confrontations with representatives of various Jewish groups in the Temple conflict stories of 11:27–12:34.[70]

The dramatic and profoundly shocking image of the rending of the Temple curtain immediately after "Jesus gave a loud cry and breathed his last" (15:37-38) is, itself, an image of the end of a symbol system. In his article on the Temple theme in Mark, John Paul Heil concludes that through his death and resurrection, Jesus builds a new temple, not made by human hands, but by the power of God. For Heil, the presence of women and Gentile Christians illustrates the inclusion of all people in the new sanctuary.[71] The "new sanctuary" (the community of Jesus believers) *is* "the house of prayer for all nations."

For Mark, the fundamental "alternative symbol" is the cross. Mark *is* a passion story with an extended introduction. Robert Gundry is correct in asserting that Mark's gospel is an "apology for the cross."[72] The "alternative symbolic universe" suggested by Mark is found precisely in the kind of Messiah Jesus is, and that is defined by his death on the cross. The cross shatters idolatrous images of God's Messiah. Mark's spokesman for the disciples, Peter, apparently did not expect a Messiah who would suffer, be rejected, and be killed (8:27-33). The disciples did not expect the servant Messiah Jesus described in the house in Capernaum (9:33-35). They probably had in mind something like the rulers of the Gentiles, great ones who "lorded it over" and "exercised authority over" their subjects, not the servant and the slave Jesus describes to James and John (10:4-45). Mark's Messiah is not self-assertive but self-denying, a concept that occurs repeatedly in the literature of asceticism and defines the Christ in Philippians 2:6-11.

In his article on ascetic behavior in the ancient Mediterranean, Bruce Malina makes the case that all ascetic behaviors "entail shrinking the self."[73] The psychophysical, psychological, socialized adult self is defined culturally as a member of a group. To shrink that self is to rid it of social accretions, to dissociate from one's group of origin, and reject gaining its "prestige credentials."[74] This is not only the "attitudinal asceticism" we are considering, but very close to what the Christ Hymn in Philippians 2:6-11, which I take to be the earliest statement of Christology, calls *kenosis*. Though Jesus was "in the form of God," he "emptied himself" and took the form of a slave (Phil 2:6-7). This radical "shrinking of the self," this emptying, led to "death on a cross" (Phil 2:8).

At the center of Mark's new symbolic universe is the ascetic self-emptying of discipleship dramatically enacted in the crucifixion of Jesus. As Morna Hooker notes, "The belief that God is revealed in the shame and weakness of the cross is a profound insight into the nature of God."[75] And, I would add, of God's Messiah. It is also the inauguration of a new understanding of the universe, with a new symbol at its center. The cross is central to Mark's "alternative symbolic universe." Jesus on the cross is, to use John Donahue's striking phrase, "the parable of God." Donahue notes that response to parables "puts the ordinary askew."[76] As with Jesus' verbal/narrative parables, not everyone "gets it." Indeed, the capacity to understand such a parable varies from person to person (4:11-12, 33-34). The reasons why this is so is another study for another time.

Valantasis closes his study on constructions of power in asceticism with the statement, "Ascetic reality is by definition a resistant reality within a dominant system."[77] In discussing primitive Christianity as an ascetic movement, Duncan Derrett remarks that "The Way expects . . . an opting out of the standards of the world into which one is born."[78] To opt out of the "normal" or expected patterns of religion, state, kinship, politics is *ipso facto* to challenge and affront those patterns and the persons who haven't raised questions about them or who benefit from following them.[79] If you have invested your life in gaining possessions, prestige, and power in a particular system (like a political party, university, or Christian de-nomination), you aren't likely to want to have the system challenged, certainly not to hear that it is sick unto death. That Jesus "opts out" and invites others to join him in doing so sets up the tension that leads to the cross. At the heart of Mark's gospel is a picture of just how dangerous "attitudinal asceticism" can be. As David Watson so eloquently wrote, "To follow Jesus is simultaneously to align oneself with the divine will and to reject basic widespread assumptions and practices. . . . To continue to hold these widespread assumptions and to go on with 'business as usual' is to reject Jesus, and thus to reject God."[80]

Conclusion

Did Mark set out to write a treatise on asceticism? No more so than he did to write a gospel focused on economic justice. Does his gospel reflect ascetic practices and attitudes present in the religious environment of the time? I hope I have made a good case that it does. In the final analysis, I agree with Anthony Saldarini writing on asceticism in Matthew that Jesus' compassion for human need is more focal than "the necessity of human discipline and abne-gation,"[81] and with Mary Ann Tolbert who wrote on asceticism in Mark that while Jesus exhibits "status asceticism" in giving up conventional family and social patterns, he is "a living symbol of plenty, just as the Kingdom of God itself is the advent of the abun-dant harvest."[82] Jesus was "the embodiment of abundance in the midst of scarcity," and for the marginal, abundance, not scarcity, was good news.[83]

So what is the implication of "Br. Jesus" in Mark? The asceti-cism in Mark's gospel brings into clear focus the radicality and countercultural message of Jesus, for which in this chapter I have been using *basilea tou theou* as shorthand and "maverick Mark" as a champion. As a narrative theologian, Mark shows us practices and attitudes of Jesus that radically challenge the status quo. Much of what falls under the rubric "discipleship" in Mark fits neatly into one of the templates for asceticism. As Eduard Schweizer noted many years ago, Mark structures his gospel around three points: (1) Jesus' rejection; (2) the call to follow Jesus; (3) the impossibility of understanding Jesus without the cross.[84] I suggest Jesus was rejected because of what I have called "attitudinal asceticism." It was his clear-eyed and unvarnished criticism of "the way things are" that led to the cross. And it is to something very similar that Jesus calls disciples.

For me, the images of asceticism in Mark's gospel point toward the inclusion and abundance of the *basilea tou theou* which, at the outset of the gospel, Jesus declares "at hand" or "near" (1:15). I hope I have shown that discipleship as Mark's Jesus exemplifies and describes it has a great deal in common with asceticism both as practice and as attitude. I think both challenge us to abstain from worshipping the great idols of this culture: possessions, prestige, and power. To refuse obeisance to them as Jesus did is to be a maverick. I agree with Vaage that discipleship in Mark is ascetical and "a process of unlearning."[85] Stephen Ahearn-Kroll concludes his recent study on inclusion and exclusion in Mark: "ultimately, discipleship for Mark requires participation in a lifestyle rather than profession of a set of propositions."[86] The "lifestyle" of discipleship in Mark looks to me suspiciously like traditional descriptions of Christian asceticism, especially if we accept the arguments of Valantasis and of Patterson that asceticism is as much a critical attitude toward dominant culture as it is any particular set of practices. Thus Patterson asserts, "The ascetic is one who ventures . . . a newly imagined reality, drawing others to it in a radical display of otherness."[87]

In our day and age anything like discipleship as Mark's gospel depicts it is pretty much a display of "radical otherness," the action of a maverick. Part of the "otherness" is knowing that what is doesn't have to be. As we find them in Mark's gospel, discipleship and asceticism invite us, albeit in the shadow of the cross, to re-envision the future in hope. Discipleship is living the reality that change is possible, although, as Gandhian teaching goes, the first call is to *become* the change we envision. Vaage's work on asceticism highlights "Mark's conviction that the proper and most effective way to enter the Kingdom of God is by redoing life at home. This may be the evangelist's most enduring challenge to us."[88]

Considering asceticism as a set of practices, or as an attitude of, if not criticism, at least skepticism about the "givens" of social, political, economic, religious life, gives us another lens through which to see the grace-filled, benevolent, and abundant alternative to the way things are that Mark's Jesus proclaimed and embodied. I think the more clearly we can see and understand it, the more we will be able to nurture it in our own lives and communities. And that, until Jesus comes again, seems to me the point of it all.

Epilogue

Readers who persevered through these chapters soon realized that their author is not objective about the material, not a coolly detached, omniscient observer of Mark's Jesus story. She is someone who is passionate about the message of Mark's Jesus who was himself as passionate as the prophets of his own tradition and with whom we might associate his preaching. This author is someone struggling along in the journey of discipleship, and from her struggle has emerged with both a clear sense of its value and an abhorrence of attempts to "water down" or domesticate a vision which, like her home state, is wild and wonderful. The point of view in this book resonates with Nick Cave's article in *Harper's Magazine*, "A Punk Rocker's Angry Christ": "Mark's Gospel is a clatter of bones . . . raw, nervy, and lean on information."[1] Cave continues, "The Christ that the church offers us, the bloodless, placid 'savior' . . . denies Christ the potent, creative sorrow of his boiling anger, which confronts us so forcefully in Mark."[2] In my view Christ has reason to be angry with what we have made of his message.

It is fair to ask in closing, "What's the take-away?"[3] I suggest two interrelated points: discipleship (which includes economics and asceticism) and "sight." Mark's is the gospel of discipleship, and "sight" is his metaphor for understanding what it means to "follow" Jesus. For Mark, discipleship is not a matter of a single event in which one "gets saved," although discipleship may begin with a singular, even dramatic, response to a call from Jesus. (See

1:16-20 or 2:13-14.) Discipleship is committing oneself to a process, to following the Leader on a journey no matter where it leads. (See 15:40-41.) It led Jesus to Calvary. As Cave notes, "when Christ takes on his ministry around Galilee and in Jerusalem, he enters a wilderness of soul, where all the outpourings of his brilliant, jewel-like imagination are . . . misunderstood, rebuffed, ignored, mocked and vilified, and would eventually be the death of him."[4] "Christ . . . was the victim of humanity's lack of imagination, was hammered to the cross with the nails of creative vapidity."[5]

In what has now become a spiritual classic, *When the Well Runs Dry*, Fr. Thomas S. Green, SJ, writes of the choices and challenges of discipleship. Green explains, "One can accept the Gospel demands or one can freely 'go away,' but one can never make them more popular, reasonable, palatable, and still follow Jesus Christ."[6] Peter "stays with Jesus not because he has found his words reasonable, but because he has found God in him."[7] Green makes clear that the "demands of faith can never be made reasonable in the sense of palatable, digestible by our human reason and our feelings" and quotes Bonhoeffer's dictum, "When God calls man, he bids him come and die."[8] In short, discipleship is not a pleasant pastime for an otherwise unplanned Sunday, but, to paraphrase the travel brochures, the trip of a lifetime.

One begins the journey of discipleship blind, or with very partial sight, but in the course of the journey, the Leader corrects and improves the disciple's sight by means of the journey itself. Even partial sight is a blessing to a blind person. But it is not good enough for the Leader who works to perfect sight/understanding. Stephen Ahearne-Kroll describes the process perfectly:

> Discipleship for Mark is not construed as assent to a series of faith propositions or the full acquisition and understanding of divine mysteries. It is predicated on becoming connected with Jesus by following him after his call and acting like him because he is the manifestation of the kingdom on earth. One learns the mystery of the kingdom through the action of following after the one who

manifests it. Insider status comes from following after Jesus, from being "around" Jesus (cf. 3:32), from becoming family of Jesus by doing the will of God (cf. 3:35), from following Jesus by picking up one's cross (cf. 8:34), from enduring until the end (cf. 3:13).[9]

Nick Cave connects the dots between Jesus and discipleship when he writes, "The essential humanness of Mark's Christ provides us with a blueprint for our own lives, so that we have something that we can aspire to."[10] As such, discipleship calls for decision, many decisions over many years. As Hans Urs von Balthasar so succinctly noted, Jesus' call is "to conversion, not to success."[11] Therefore, one decision the modern disciple must make is whether to live from a model of scarcity or of abundance. The economic system in the West, as it certainly was in the Roman Empire, is basically a "scarcity" system. If there isn't enough to go around, then one's basic task is to acquire, to get enough. Indeed, to amass a superfluity and hoard it constitutes "success." But if there is an abundance, then the task is to distribute the profusion. If one wishes to discern something of Kingdom economics in Mark, then it is useful to read his gospel asking the following question of any given story: "In this pericope does Jesus assume scarcity or abundance?"

In engaging in this exercise myself, I came to conclusions very similar to those of Mary Ann Tolbert. She writes that "For Mark, Jesus is a living symbol of plenty, just as the Kingdom of God itself is the advent of the abundant harvest (4:8, 20)."[12] The picture of the Kingdom of God in Mark's gospel, and of Jesus himself, are images of abundance. Even "appearances to the contrary," to live in the Kingdom is to live in God's abundance. And if there is enough, not only enough material "stuff," but enough grace and mercy and love and all the virtues and gifts that the Kingdom offers, then perhaps our economic problem is not amount but distribution. As Tolbert asserts, for the marginal, abundance, not scarcity, was good news.[13]

Clearly (I hope!), what I am describing is another aspect of "sight," specifically, the ability to see things differently, to envision other ways of thinking and being and doing in the world. Jesus' embodiment of the Kingdom, his intention for his small band of disciples, was that they would be little glimpses of other ways of being and doing. That is really the only point I was making in chapter 4. For example, the unusual table fellowship of Jesus which I highlighted many times in this volume is an example of his inclusive vision. As Neufeld explains, "Table fellowship. . .symbolizes the establishment of relationships based not so much on the conventions of social stratification as on a radically inclusive companionship in which boundaries between people are being broken down."[14] Or the renunciation of conventional family patterns which we examined in chapter 4, what Tolbert calls "status asceticism,"[15] is another image of a different, a radically different, way to be in the world.

So is the "way it is," the status quo, always bad? Are all conventional patterns "evil"? *Ipso facto*, of course not. But they might be if they take precedence over the patterns suggested for subjects in the Kingdom of God. Jesus continues to call people to "another way" beyond culturally accepted norms and givens, to a more compassionate, inclusive, and "just" (i.e., "righteous") way of being in the world. The cross of Christ is the symbol of this reordering. Taken seriously, it is very likely to drive one "outside the camp."

Leif E. Vaage's definition of "asceticism" very nearly fits my current understanding (remember I am still on the journey) of what it means to be a disciple of Jesus, a citizen of the Kingdom of God. It rejects the world as normative and discovers and *enjoys* (and this is crucial to the program because Jesus came to give life and joy) what is desired as a result. It is "to live 'against the grain' of whatever is taken to be distractingly or deceptively normative in a given cultural context, in order to experience here and now . . . a better or 'larger' life."[16] John's Jesus says, "I came that they may have life, and *have it abundantly*" (John 10:10, italics mine). It is not that "the world" or any given culture is "bad," but that, in every case, the Kingdom of God which Jesus proclaimed is better. And the interesting thing is, one can be a citizen of God's Kingdom *in the world*. It is noteworthy that in what is often called his "High Priestly Prayer," John's Jesus does not ask God to take his followers "out of the world" but "to protect them from the evil one" (John 17:15), whose infection and influence is distressingly prevalent in the world and its "accepted patterns."

Mark's gospel and the discipleship to which Jesus calls his followers require that we see him as something other than the "gentle Child of gentle Mother" of the children's hymn.[17] In a reflection in *Give Us This Day*, Mary Katharine Deeley gets it just right: "Jesus is so much seen as the face of the God of love that we forget his reputation as a disturber of the peace, a thorn in the side of the establishment, and the one who challenges our complacency and self-righteousness. . . . If Jesus is tamed, then we do not have to hold ourselves accountable for our sin or sacrifice our lives."[18]

In fact, Jesus' Galilean disciples as Mark depicted them are still paradigmatic for us. Called from their ordinary, daily work, they follow. Embarrassingly frequently they misunderstand the Leader and what he says and does. But they keep following. Some of them stay right up to his bitter end on the cross. Eventually they go home to be and to make disciples there. This is why the young man whom Mary Magdalene and Mary the mother of James and Salome meet at the empty tomb charges them, "go, tell his disciples and Peter that he is going ahead of you to Galilee; *there you will see him*" (16:7, italics mine). Peter, symbol of the uncomprehending and even denying disciples, is "rehabilitated." And the promise is that Jesus will meet them all in Galilee, at home, locus of the "same old same old" daily grind. In Mark's untamed gospel, discipleship and Kingdom economics and revisioning continue at home. Indeed, this is why Jesus did not allow the Gerasene demoniac whom he exorcised to accompany him, but charged him to "Go home to your friends, and tell them how much the Lord has done for you, and what mercy he has shown you" (Mark 5:19). As Vaage so perceptively writes, the "alternative life of faith . . . returns home again, in order to live there otherwise."[19] "Galilee," "home" is where Kingdom happens. Or doesn't.

This is why I think the very odd ending of Mark's gospel at 16:8 is his intended one. His is a gospel written for a community under siege, a community suffering for being an outpost of God's Kingdom. So while Mark's gospel presupposes the resurrection (remember the three passion predictions in chaps. 9–10), Mark's Jesus is understood in terms of the cross. Mark depicts the faithful women disciples with a heavenly messenger in an empty tomb, but not a resurrection appearance of Jesus. Mark leaves the reader with the cross because that was where his community stood: facing their crosses. As A. T. Lincoln points out, the juxtaposition of verses 7 and 8 are Mark's paradigm of Christian existence. There is a word of promise, and there is the failure of the human disciples. But the word of promise predominates. If the disciples and witnesses fail (and they do), the message and the cause is not lost.[20]

The ending of Mark's gospel is really a beginning, the "return home," if you will. It reminds us that fear as well as faith is an essential note of Christian discipleship.[21] (Thus, Jesus' "cry of dereliction" from the cross in 15:34.) It reminds us that resurrection is God's way of affirming Jesus' at the end, but crucifixion can be God's way in the world for those who "envision differently," those who struggle to "follow" Jesus right into the Kingdom of God. To confess Jesus as Messiah is to confess him as the King on the Cross which is why, in Mark's gospel, the confession that Jesus is a Son of God comes only at his death by crucifixion and on the lips of a Gentile centurion, the outsider who is his executioner. In spite of the disciples' fearful denial and silence, there is the renewed promise of Christ that he will meet them in Galilee, the home to which they return and can never be the same again.

We disciples are to be like the women at the tomb. We follow. We see differently. We are given a new vision and a message to declare. If we fall or fail, it only matters if we don't get up and start over. We begin again. And again. And again. Perhaps maverick Mark's most outrageous message is that personal failure isn't all that important. Jesus "failed" in crucifixion, and *because of* that was raised up and started again. With us.

Notes

Prologue

1. See the first book in the series, *The Lion, the Witch and the Wardrobe*: "He's wild, you know. Not like a *tame* lion" ([London: Penguin Books, 1950, 1969], 166). See also the last book in the series, *The Last Battle*: "He is not a Tame Lion" ([London: Penguin Books, 1956, 1969], 20). Readers may also find Rowan Williams' *The Lion's World: A Journey into the Heart of Narnia* (London, SPCK, 2012) of interest.

2. Scholarly consensus is that the most original manuscripts of Mark end: "they said nothing to anyone, for they were afraid" (16:8).

3. Annie Dillard, *Teaching a Stone to Talk: Expeditions and Encounters* (New York: Harper & Row, 1982), 40–41.

4. Morna D. Hooker, *Not Ashamed of the Gospel: New Testament Interpretations of the Death of Christ* (Grand Rapids, MI: Eerdmans, 1995), 8–9, 12.

5. Robert H. Gundry, *Mark: A Commentary on His Apology for the Cross* (Grand Rapids, MI: Eerdmans, 1993).

6. Hooker, *Not Ashamed of the Gospel*, 48.

7. Ibid., 140–41.

8. Ibid., 67.

9. Gundry, *Mark*, 3.

10. N. T. Wright, *Mark for Everyone* (Louisville, KY: Westminster John Knox Press, 2004), 149.

11. Robert Kysar, *John, the Maverick Gospel* (Louisville, KY: Westminster John Knox Press, 1976; 3rd ed., 2007).

12. *Merriam-Webster's Collegiate Dictionary*, 10th ed. (Springfield, MA: Merriam-Webster, Inc., 1994), s.v. "maverick."

Chapter 1

1. James Hoover, *Mark: Follow Me* (Downers Grove, IL: InterVarsity Press, 1985), 8.

2. For an interesting and helpful reading of this text, see Harry Fledderman, "The Flight of a Naked Young Man," *Catholic Biblical Quarterly* 41 (1979), 412–18.

3. See, for example, John R. Donahue, "Windows and Mirrors: The Setting of Mark's Gospel," *Catholic Biblical Quarterly* 57, no. 1 (1995): 1–26, and Joel Marcus, "The Jewish War and the *Sitz im Leben* of Mark," *Journal of Biblical Literature* 3 (1992): 441–62.

4. Marcus makes a strong case for Roman Syria around 70 AD. See note 3 above.

5. It was suggested to me that "Palestinian Christianity" is a problematic term. Jesus the Jew grew up in the Galilean town of Nazareth in the Roman Empire's province of Palestine. "Roman Palestine" was the term used by my professor of New Testament Backgrounds, Helmut Koester, at Harvard Divinity School. (See his *Introduction to the New Testament*, vol. 2 [Philadelphia: Fortress Press, 1982].) It is the term preferred in the period maps in *The Oxford Bible Atlas* (New York: Oxford University Press, 1990) and is used without reference to modern political entities by many contemporary New Testament scholars to designate a geographical region in the Greco-Roman (or at least part of the Second Temple) period.

6. C. H. Dodd, *The Founder of Christianity* (New York: Collins/Fontana Books, 1970), 46.

7. Robert H. Gundry, *Mark: A Commentary on His Apology for the Cross* (Grand Rapids, MI: Eerdmans, 1993).

8. To my mind, this is the basic argument of St. Paul in the Philippian letter.

9. For a metaphorical reading of Mark's geography, see Bonnie B. Thurston, *The Spiritual Landscape of Mark* (Collegeville, MN: Liturgical Press, 2008).

10. For interesting readings of this material, see Elizabeth Struthers Malbon, "The Poor Widow in Mark and His Poor Rich Readers," *Catholic Biblical Quarterly* 53 (1991): 589–604, and Addison G. Wright, "The Widow's Mites: Praise or Lament?—A Matter of Context," *Catholic Biblical Quarterly* 44 (1982): 256–65.

11. J. D. Kingsbury, "The Religious Authorities in the Gospel of Mark," *New Testament Studies* 36 (1990): 62.

12. John Paul Heil, "The Narrative Strategy and Pragmatics of the Temple Theme in Mark," *Catholic Biblical Quarterly* 59 (1997): 76–100.

13. Sharyn E. Dowd, *Prayer, Power, and the Problem of Suffering: Mark 11:22-25 in the Context of Markan Theology*, SBL Dissertation Series 105 (Atlanta, GA: Scholar's Press, 1988).

14. Elizabeth Struthers Malbon's illuminating book, *In the Company of Jesus: Characters in Mark's Gospel* (Louisville, KY: Westminster John Knox Press, 2000), treats this matter in detail.

15. Paul J. Achtemeier, "Mark, Gospel of," in *The Anchor Bible Dictionary*, vol. 4 (New York: Doubleday, 1992), 4:553.

16. For a highly readable study, see Wilfrid J. Harrington, *Jesus Our Brother: The Humanity of the Lord* (New York: Paulist Press, 2010). A more demanding work that uses Mark extensively is Gerhard Lohfink, *Jesus of Nazareth: What He Wanted, Who He Was* (Collegeville, MN: Liturgical Press, 2012).

17. Stephen P. Ahearne-Kroll, "Audience Inclusion and Exclusion as Rhetorical Technique in the Gospel of Mark," *Journal of Biblical Literature* 129, no. 4 (2010): 734–35.

18. Joseph Cardinal Bernardin, *The Gift of Peace* (Chicago: Loyola Press, 1997), 48–49, quoted in *Give Us This Day*, 2, no. 3 (March 2012): 271.

19. Anthony J. Gittins, *Give Us This Day*, 2, no. 3 (March 2012): 260.

Chapter 2

1. This chapter is an expanded version of my Dean E. Walker Lecture sponsored by the European Evangelistic Society and given at the General Assembly of the Christian Church (Disciples of Christ) October 19, 2003, Charlotte, NC. It was privately published by the E.E.S. as pamphlet GA-10, and I am grateful for permission to use the original material here.

2. Adela Yarbro Collins, *Mark: A Commentary*, Hermeneia: A Critical and Historical Commentary on the Bible (Minneapolis, MN: Fortress Press, 2007); John R. Donahue and Daniel J. Harrington, *The Gospel of Mark*, Sacra Pagina Series (Collegeville, MN: Liturgical Press, 2002); Francis J. Moloney, *The Gospel of Mark: A Commentary* (Peabody, MA: Hendrickson, 2002); Joel Marcus, *Mark 1–8: A New Translation with Introduction and Commentary*, Anchor Bible Commentaries (New York: Doubleday, 2000), and *Mark 8–16: A New Translation and Commentary*, Anchor Bible Commentaries (New York: Doubleday, 2009).

3. Brian K. Blount and Gary W. Charles, *Preaching Mark in Two Voices* (Louisville, KY: Westminster John Knox Press, 2002); Bonnie Thurston, *Preaching Mark* (Minneapolis, MN: Fortress, 2002).

4. Ernest Best, *Disciples and Discipleship: Studies in the Gospel According to Mark* (Edinburgh: T. & T. Clark, 1986).

5. M. Kahler quoted in Heinz-Dieter Knigge, "The Meaning of Mark," *Interpretation* 22 (1968): 68.

6. Paul Achtemeier, "Mark as Interpreter of the Jesus Traditions," *Interpretation* 32 (1978): 340.

7. Best, *Disciples and Discipleship*, 2.

8. Marie Noël Keller, "Opening Blind Eyes: A Revisioning of Mark 8:22–10:52," *Biblical Theology Bulletin* 31, no. 4 (2001): 152.

9. See the explanation in chapter 1 on pp. 7–9.

10. A particularly clear redactional look at this material is found in Norman Perrin, *What Is Redaction Criticism?* (Philadelphia: Fortress Press, 1969/1984), chapter 3, especially pp. 50–57. My understanding and discussion of this material owes a great deal to Perrin's thought.

11. Elizabeth S. Malbon, "Fallible Followers: Women and Men in the Gospel of Mark," *Semeia* 28 (1983): 41.

12. Earl S. Johnson Jr., "Mark 10:46-52: Blind Bartimaeus," *Catholic Biblical Quarterly* 40 (1978): 201. And for further elucidation of this pericope, see Vernon K. Robbins, "The Healing of Blind Bartimaeus (10:46-52) in Marcan Theology," *Journal of Biblical Literature* 92 (1973): 224–43, and M. G. Steinhauser, "The Form of the Bartimaeus Narrative (Mark 10:46-52)," *New Testament Studies* 32 (1986): 583–95.

13. Achtemeier, "Mark as Interpreter," 348.

14. Mary Ann Beavis, "From the Margin to the Way: a Feminist Reading of the Story of Bartimaeus," *Journal of Feminist Studies in Religion* 14 (Spring 1998): 10–39.

15. A vast periodical literature from across the theological spectrum has developed on the interpretation of this pericope. Representative articles include T. A. Burkill, "The Historical Development of the Story of the Syro-Phoenician Woman," *Novum Testamentum* 9 (1967): 161–77; H. Kinukawa, *Women and Jesus in Mark: A Japanese Feminist Perspective* (Maryknoll, NY: Orbis, 1994), chapter 3; P. Pokorny, "From a Puppy to the Child: Some Problems of Contemporary Biblical Exegesis Demonstrated from Mark 7.24-30/Matt 15.21-8," *New Testament Studies* 41

(1995): 321–27; D. Rhoads, "Jesus and the Syrophoenician Woman in Mark: A Narrative-Critical Study," *Journal of the American Academy of Religion* 62 (1994): 343–71; J. M. Gundry-Volf and Miroslav Volf, *A Spacious Heart: Essays on Identity and Belonging* (Harrisburg, PA: Trinity Press, 1997), 21–32.

16. See, for starters, William Wrede, *The Messianic Secret* (Cambridge: James Clarke, 1971). Many scholars who do not agree with his interpretation still use the phrase.

17. D. E. Nineham, *Saint Mark* (London: Penguin, 1963), 217.

18. Ibid.

19. Judges 9:7-15 is a biblical parallel. There also exists an inscription from Epidaurus recording a cure in the Aesclepion in which Alcetas of Halice was cured of blindness and first saw trees. (Recorded in Nineham, *Saint Mark*, 219.) Similarly, Tacitus, *Hist.*, 4:81, Suetonius, *Vesp.*, 7.2-3, and Dio Cassius 66.8 report that Vespasian (9–79 AD and thus a contemporary of Jesus and Mark) healed a blind man in Alexandria with saliva.

20. R. S. Sugirtharajah provides a helpful summary of possibilities in "Men, Trees and Walking: A Conjectural Solution to Mk 8:24," *Expository Times* 103 (1991): 172–74.

21. Ibid., 174.

22. As Morna D. Hooker suggests in her commentary, *The Gospel According to St. Mark*, Black's New Testament Commentary (Peabody, MA: Hendrickson, 1991), 198.

23. For more on this point, see Jarl Fossum, "Understanding Jesus' Miracles," *BR* 10 (1994): 16–23, 50.

24. Donahue and Harrington, *The Gospel of Mark*, 256.

25. Ibid., 257.

26. Mary Ann Tolbert, "How the Gospel of Mark Builds Character," *Interpretation* 47 (1993): 348.

27. Best, *Disciples and Discipleship*, 102.

28. Helpful readings of the passage are found in A. A. Trites, "The Transfiguration of Jesus: The Gospel in Microcosm," *Evangelical Quarterly* 51 (1979): 67–79; E. Best, "The Markan Redaction of the Transfiguration," in *Disciples and Discipleship*, 206–25; J. Murphy-O'Connor, "What Really Happened at the Transfiguration?" *BR* 3 (1987): 8–21.

29. For more on Jesus and exorcism, see G. Sterling, "Jesus as Exorcist," *Catholic Biblical Quarterly* 55 (1993): 467–93.

30. For readings of this text, see Barbara Green, "Jesus' Teaching on Divorce in the Gospel of Mark," *Journal for the Study of the New Testament* 38 (1990): 67–75, and Robert W. Herron, "Mark's Jesus on Divorce: Mark 10:1-12 Reconsidered," *Journal of the Evangelical Theological Society* 25 (1982): 273–81.

31. In her book *The Misunderstood Jew: The Church and the Scandal of the Jewish Jesus* (San Francisco: Harper One, 2007), Amy-Jill Levine has pointed out that "In the popular Christian imagination, Jesus still remains defined, incorrectly and unfortunately, as 'against' the Law, or at least against how it was understood at the time; as 'against' the Temple as an institution and not simply against its first-century leadership; as 'against' the people Israel but in favor of the Gentiles" (19). This study does not suggest that Jesus was anti-Jewish. He was a Jew, and as Professor Levine points out, "Jesus's connections to the basic Jewish teachings were right on target" (21). However unfortunate it may be for modern Jewish-Christian relations, it is the case that to some extent, for Mark the evangelist, "Judaism becomes . . . a negative foil" (19), a matter Levine's work eloquently addresses.

The discussion at this point is about ritual purity "a means of sanctifying the body, resisting assimilation, showing discipline . . . and following Torah." (Quoted from an e-mail from Dr. Levine, December 24, 2012.) Interestingly, Mark's gospel reflects what Stephen Westerholm's entry in *Dictionary of Jesus and the Gospels* (Downer's Grove, IL: InterVarsity Press, 1992, pp. 125–32) discusses as "postexilic sensitivity to the need for purity" (127). Westerholm writes, "It is largely in postexilic literature that issues of ritual purity play a significant role," and, "it was particularly among sectarian groups . . . that observance of purity laws was rigorous and consistent" (127). He mentions, in particular, Essenes, the Qumran Sect, and Pharisees.

Jesus would not have viewed ritual purity (or the Temple in Jerusalem for that matter) as inherently evil. For example, at the outset of his public ministry Jesus tells a cured leper to observe "what Moses commanded" (Mark 1:44). Mark's depiction of Jesus' conversations with the Pharisees about purity is not because ritual purity was evil but because it was important. As Levine points out in her discussion of the Sermon on the Mount, "Jesus does not 'oppose' the Law; he extends it" (47). But, as Westerholm notes, "Mark's gospel does not share the vision which inspired the pursuit of ritual purity. For Mark's Gentile readers Jewish purity concerns are foreign (7:3-4)" (129–30). "One of the major debates in the early church was not whether Jews who followed Jesus needed to keep kosher, but whether Gentiles who followed him needed to do so as well" (Levine, 26).

Or, to give another example, I point out that in the composition of his gospel, Mark used Jerusalem and the Temple as *symbols* of opposition to Jesus. Our reading of the gospel must be intelligently nuanced enough to recognize this didn't make either *inherently* evil. Levine notes, "Historically, Jesus should be seen as continuous with the line of *Jewish teachers and prophets*" (20). Exactly so. And more than one prophet of Israel was critical of its beloved and revered Temple. Like those Jewish teachers and prophets in whose lineage he stands, Jesus may be best viewed as the "loyal opposition," indeed, as I suggest in this book, one who, like the prophets, calls his tradition to its own highest ideals. And in this role "Jesus would have expected to be challenged, and he would have issued his own challenges" (29).

32. Best, *Disciples and Discipleship*, 3.

33. Ibid., 186.

34. Hooker, *Gospel*, 197.

35. Donahue and Harrington, *The Gospel of Mark*, 257.

36. Keller, "Opening Blind Eyes," 151–57.

37. Ibid., 156–57.

38. David Hawkin, "The Incomprehension of the Disciples in the Marcan Redaction," *Journal of Biblical Literature* 91 (1982): 491.

39. R. C. Tannehill, "The Disciples in Mark: The Function of a Narrative Role," *Journal of Religion* 57 (1977): 386–405.

40. J. F. Williams, "Other Followers of Jesus: Minor Characters as Major Figures in Mark's Gospel," *Journal for the Study of the New Testament*, ser. 102 (1994): 117–21. Also see Struthers Malbon's book mentioned above.

41. I suggest John uses the same technique in his gospel.

42. This point is made by both J. B. Tyson in "The Blindness of the Disciples in Mark," *Journal of Biblical Literature* 80 (1961): 262, and Hawkin, *The Incomprehension*, 492.

43. Eduard Schweizer, "The Portrayal of the Life of Faith in the Gospel of Mark," *Interpretation* 32 (1978): 387–99.

44. Donahue and Harrington, *The Gospel of Mark*, 258.

45. Moloney, *The Gospel of Mark*, 164.

46. Donahue and Harrington, *The Gospel of Mark*, 258.

Chapter 3

1. This chapter originated as a talk for Christian Associates of South West Pennsylvania's Third Annual Preaching Seminar given November 3, 2005, at Pittsburgh Theological Seminary, Pittsburgh, Pennsylvania. A version was included in a privately duplicated collection of essays in honor of the fortieth annual Institute on Sacred Scripture sponsored by Misericordia University, Dallas, PA. It is used here with knowledge and permission of its editor, Dr. Marie Noël Keller.

2. As this book was going to press, I learned of an article on a similar topic by respected and admired Markan scholar, Fr. John R. Donahue, SJ. As a more nuanced treatment of this theme, I highly recommend his chapter, "The Lure of Wealth: Does Mark Have a Social Gospel?," in *Unity and Diversity in the New Testament: Essays in Honor of Frank J. Matera*, ed. Christopher W. Skinner and Kelly B. Iverson (Atlanta, GA: Society of Biblical Literature, 2012), 71–93.

3. Thomas Merton, "A Letter to Pablo Antonio Cuadra Concerning Giants," in *The Collected Poems of Thomas Merton* (New York: New Directions, 1977), 384.

4. Barclay M. Newman Jr., *A Concise Greek-English Dictionary of the New Testament* (London: United Bible Societies, 1971), 46.

5. Scot McKnight, "Justice, Righteousness" in *Dictionary of Jesus and the Gospels*, ed. Joel B. Green and Scot McKnight (Downers Grove, IL: InterVarsity Press, 1992), 412. Hereafter in notes as DJG.

6. Ibid., 411.

7. A classic study of Hellenism which has gone through many editions is W. W. Tarn and G. T. Griffith, *Hellenistic Civilisation* (London: Edward Arnold, Ltd., 1927, 1959). A more recent work which includes excellent bibliography is Helmut Koester, *Introduction to the New Testament*, vol. 1: *History, Culture, and Religion of the Hellenistic Age* (Philadelphia: Fortress Press, 1982).

8. An excellent and very readable history of this period is Donald E. Gowan, *Bridge between the Testaments: A Reappraisal of Judaism from the Exile to the Birth of Christianity*, Pittsburgh Theological Monograph Series 14 (Pittsburgh, PA: Pickwick Press, 1976). See also Werner Foerster, *From the Exile to Christ: Historical Introduction to Palestinian Judaism*, trans. Gordon E. Harris (Philadelphia: Fortress Press, 1964/74).

9. An older but very accessible picture of the economics of Jerusalem at the time of Jesus is Joachim Jeremias' *Jerusalem in the Time of Jesus* (Philadelphia: Fortress Press, 1975), part 2, "Economic Status."

10. John E. Stambaugh and David L. Balch, *The New Testament in Its Social Environment* (Philadelphia: Westminster John Knox Press, 1986), 63.

11. Ibid., 65. For more on coinage and monetary systems in the period, see Koester, *Introduction to the New Testament*, part 2, section 7, "Trade, Monetary Systems, and Banking"; 2.7c treats coinage.

12. Richard L. Rohrbaugh, "The Social Location of the Markan Audience," *Interpretation* 47, no. 4 (1993): 383–88.

13. On agriculture in the period, see Koester, *Introduction to the New Testament*, part 2, section 5 "Agriculture."

14. Rohrbaugh, "The Social Location," 389.

15. Stambaugh and Balch, *The New Testament*, 66.

16. For more information on fishing, see "Fishing Nets" in *Jesus and His World: An Archaelogical and Cultural Dictionary*, ed. John J. Rousseau and Rami Arav (Minneapolis, MN: Fortress Press, 1995), 93–97.

17. On manufacturing and industry, see Koester, *Introduction to the New Testament*, part 2, section 5.

18. One of the most interesting studies on urban life in Greco-Roman cities is Abraham J. Malherbe's *Paul and the Thessalonians: The Philosophical Tradition of Pastoral Care* (Philadelphia: Fortress Press, 1987).

19. Stambaugh and Balch, *The New Testament*, 65.

20. For more on slavery, see S. Scott Bartchy, "Slavery, NT," *Anchor Bible Dictionary* (New York: Doubleday, 1992), 6:65–73; William L. Westermann, *The Slave Systems of Greek and Roman Antiquity* (Philadelphia: The American Philosophical Society, 1955). For the particular problems posed for Christians by slavery, see J. Barclay, "Paul, Philemon, and the Dilemma of Christian Slave Ownership," *New Testament Studies* 36, no. 2 (1991): 161–86.

21. Stambaugh and Balch, *The New Testament*, 76.

22. P. H. Davids, "Rich and Poor" in DJG, 702.

23. For more, see "Coins and Money" and "Coins as Historical Documents" in *Jesus and His World*, 55–68.

24. Ibid., 79.

25. T. E. Schmidt, "Taxes" in DJG, 804.

26. Joachim Jeremias, *Jerusalem in the Time of Jesus* (Philadelphia: Fortress Press, 1975), 96.

27. Koester, *Introduction to the New Testament*, 1:327.

28. See John Donahue, "Tax Collectors and Sinners," *Catholic Biblical Quarterly* 33, no. 1 (1971): 39–61.

29. Schmidt, "Taxes," 806.

30. Ibid, 804.

31. "Taxes and Tax Collectors," in *Jesus and His World*, 278. See also D. C. Snell, "Taxes and Taxation," *Anchor Bible Dictionary*, 6:338–40.

32. Quoted by Catherine Murphy in her lecture, "The Alternative Economy Envisioned in the Love Commandment," given at Catholic Biblical Association of America, Saint John's University, Collegeville, Minnesota, August 7, 2005.

33. Leslie J. Hoppe, *There Shall Be No Poor among You: Poverty in the Bible* (Nashville, TN: Abindgon Press, 2004), 144.

34. Rohrbaugh, "The Social Location," 388.

35. Ibid., 392.

36. For a very interesting study of this matter, see Bernadette J. Brooten, *Women Leaders in the Ancient Synagogue: Inscriptional Evidence and Background Issues* (Chico, CA: Scholars Press, 1982).

37. Albert Nolan, *Jesus Today: A Spirituality of Radical Freedom* (Maryknoll, NY: Orbis Books, 2006), 51, quoted in Wilfrid J. Harrington, *Jesus Our Brother: The Humanity of the Lord* (New York: Paulist Press, 2010), 106 (chap. 2, note 2).

38. Joseph of Arimathea is an important figure in another way. His attention to proper burial for Jesus, and thus albeit secondarily his kindness to Jesus' family and associates, makes it clear that Mark is not anti-Jewish. Mark says he was "a respected member of the council, who was also himself waiting expectantly for the kingdom of God," and he "went *boldly* to Pilate and asked for the body of Jesus" (15:43, italics mine). Joseph knew the risks involved in the request he was making.

39. Harrington, *Jesus Our Brother*, 27.

40. Ibid., 28.

41. Jeremias, *Jerusalem*, 113–14.

42. Charles N. Giblin, " 'The Things of God' in the Question Concerning Tribute to Caesar," *Catholic Biblical Quarterly* 33 (1971): 510–13, quotation from p. 513. This story is representative of the many conflict dialogues in Mark in which people come to ask Jesus questions in order to trap him. For an interesting study, see Jerome H. Neyrey,

"Questions, *Chreiai* and Challenges to Honor: The Interface of Rhetoric and Culture in Mark's Gospel," *Catholic Biblical Quarterly* 60, no. 4 (1998): 657–81.

43. L. D. Hurst, "Ethics of Jesus" in DJG, 220.

44. Hoppe, *There Shall Be No Poor*, 146.

45. See John Paul Heil, "The Narrative Strategy and Pragmatics of the Temple Theme in Mark," *Catholic Biblical Quarterly* 59, no. 1 (1997): 76–100; Bonnie Thurston, *Preaching Mark* (Minneapolis, MN: Fortress Press, 2002), 122–24. The point is not that Jesus in this story opposes the Temple per se but that it functions as a symbol for Mark of opposition to him. See chap. 2, note 31 above.

46. Hoppe, *There Shall Be No Poor*, 164.

47. For more on this point, see Elizabeth Struthers Malbon, "The Poor Widow in Mark and Her Poor Rich Readers," *Catholic Biblical Quarterly* 53, no. 4 (1991): 589–604, and a counter view in Jeremias, *Jerusalem*, 114.

48. Harrington, *Jesus Our Brother*, 30.

49. Thomas H. Green, *When the Well Runs Dry: Prayer Beyond the Beginnings* (Notre Dame, IN: Ave Maria Press, 1979), 167.

50. Ibid.,168.

51. Hoppe, *There Shall Be No Poor*, 164.

52. P. H. Davids, "Rich and Poor" in DJG, 706.

53. Harrington, *Jesus Our Brother*, 29.

54. Ibid., 67.

55. Davids, "Rich and Poor," 704.

56. Murphy, "The Alternative Economy Envisioned in the Love Command."

57. Hurst, "Ethics of Jesus," 216.

58. Hoppe, *There Shall Be No Poor*, 164.

59. Harrington, *Jesus Our Brother*, 28.

60. Davids, "Rich and Poor," 705.

61. Hurst, "Ethics of Jesus," 214.

62. Davids, "Rich and Poor," 708. For an extended examination of this very touchy subject, see Luke Timothy Johnson, *Sharing Possessions: What Faith Demands*, 2nd ed. (Grand Rapids, MI: Eerdmans, 2011).

63. Amy-Jill Levine, *The Misunderstood Jew: The Church and the Scandal of the Jewish Jesus* (San Francisco: Harper One, 2007), 51–52.

64. For another study of "economics" in the New Testament, see Bruce W. Longenecker, *Remember the Poor: Paul, Poverty, and the Greco-Roman World* (Grand Rapids, MI: Eerdmans, 2010).

65. Davids, "Rich and Poor," 706.

66. John Koenig, *Rediscovering New Testament Prayer: Boldness and Blessing in the Name of Jesus* (Harrisburg, PA: Morehouse Publishing, 1992, 1998), 45.

Chapter 4

1. An earlier version of this material was given as an address at the Catholic Biblical Association of America meeting at Assumption College, Wooster, Massachusetts, in July 2011, and subsequently to the community at Our Lady of the Angels Monastery (Cistercian), Crozet, Virginia.

2. Dennis C. Dulling, "Kingdom of God/Kingdom of Heaven—New Testament and Early Christian Literature," in *The Anchor Bible Dictionary* (New York: Doubleday, 1992), 4:56.

3. C. C. Caragounis, *Dictionary of Jesus and the Gospels* (Downers Grove, IL: InterVarsity Press, 1992), 417 and 430; hereafter DJG.

4. Dulling, "Kingdom of God," 4:56.

5. See, for example, Vincent L. Wimbush, ed., *Ascetic Behavior in Greco-Roman Antiquity: A Sourcebook* (Minneapolis, MN: Fortress Press, 1990); Vincent L. Wimbush and Richard Valantasis, eds., *Asceticism* (Oxford: Oxford University Press, 1998); Richard Valantasis, "Constructions of Power in Asceticism," *Journal of the American Academy of Religion* 63 (1995): 775–821.

6. Hans von Campenhausen, *Tradition and Life in the Church: Essays and Lectures on Church History* (Philadelphia: Fortress, 1968).

7. J. Duncan Derrett, *The Ascetic Discourse: An Explanation of the Sermon on the Mount* (Eilsbrunn: Ko'amar, 1989).

8. Unless otherwise noted, these articles are collected in Leif E. Vaage and Vincent L. Wimbush, *Asceticism and the New Testament* (New York/London: Routledge, 1999); Robert Murray, "The Features of Earliest Christian Asceticism," in *Christian Spirituality*, ed. Peter Brooks (London: SCM Press, 1975), 63–77; Leif E. Vaage, "An Other Home: Discipleship in Mark as Domestic Asceticism," *Catholic Biblical Quarterly* 71, no. 4 (2009): 741–61; Vincent L. Wimbush, *Discursive Formations, Ascetic Piety and the Interpretation of Early Christian Literature*, 2 vols. (Atlanta, GA: Scholars Press, 1992).

9. James E. Goehring, "Asceticism," in *Encyclopedia of Early Christianity*, ed. Everett Ferguson, 2nd ed. (New York: Garland, 1990), 104.

10. H. Wimbush, "*askeo*," in *The Theological Dictionary of the New Testament: Abridged in One Volume*, ed. Gerhard Kittle and Gerhard Friedrich, trans. Geoffrey W. Bromiley (Grand Rapids, MI: Eerdmans, 1985), 84.

11. Vaage, "An Other Home," 742.

12. H. Wimbush, "*askeo*," 84.

13. F. L. Cross, "Asceticism," in *The Oxford Dictionary of the Christian Church*, ed. F. L. Cross and E. A. Livingstone (Oxford: Oxford University Press, 1997), 113.

14. W. Grundmann, "*enkretia*," in Kittle and Friedrich, *The Theological Dictionary*, 196.

15. Kallistos Ware, "The Way of the Ascetics: Negative or Affirmative?," in Wimbush and Valantasis, *Asceticism*, 3–15.

16. Stephen J. Patterson, "Askesis and the Early Jesus Tradition," in Vaage and Wimbush, *Asceticism and the New Testament*, 57.

17. James H. Moulton and George Milligan, *The Vocabulary of the Greek Testament* (Grand Rapids, MI: Eerdmans, 1980), 40.

18. Mary Ann Tolbert, "Asceticism and Mark's Gospel," in Vaage and Wimbush, *Asceticism and the New Testament*, 35–36.

19. Columba Stewart, "Christian Spirituality during the Roman Empire (100–600)," in *The Blackwell Companion to Christian Spirituality*, ed. Arthur Holder (Oxford: Blackwell Publishing, 2005), 84.

20. Goehring, "Asceticism," 106.

21. Murray, "The Features," 77.

22. Goehring, "Asceticism," 104. See Matthew Black, "The Tradition of Hasidaen-Essene Asceticism: Its Origins and Influence," *Aspects du Judeo-christianisme* (Colloque de Strasbourg, 1964), 19–33.

23. Vincent L. Wimbush, ed., *Ascetic Behavior in Greco-Roman Antiquity* (Minneapolis, MN: Fortress, 1990).

24. See, for example, Seneca, *Ep.mor,* 56.6-7.

25. Kaelber quoted in Richard Valantasis, "Constructions of Power," 794.

26. Quoted in ibid., 792.

27. Goehring, "Asceticism," 104.

28. Cross, "Asceticism," 113.

29. Stewart, "Christian Spirituality," 84.

30. Henry Chadwick, "The Ascetic Ideal in the History of the Church," in *Monks, Hermits and the Ascetic Tradition: Papers Read at the 1985 Summer Meeting and the 1985 Winter Meeting of the Ecclesiastical History Society*, ed. W. J. Sheils (Oxford: Basil Blackwell, 1985), 2.

31. Stephen J. Patterson, "Askesis and the Early Jesus Tradition," in Vaage and Wimbush, *Asceticism and the New Testament*, 65.

32. Valantasis, "Constructions," 795–96.

33. Dulling, "Kingdom of God," 4:56.

34. Ernest Best, *Disciples and Discipleship: Studies in the Gospel of Mark* (Edinburgh: T. & T. Clark, 2000), 3.

35. Von Campenhausen, *Tradition and Life*, 92.

36. Ibid.

37. Ibid., 94–95.

38. Elizabeth S. Malbon, "The Poor Widow in Mark and Her Poor Rich Readers," *Catholic Biblical Quarterly* 53, no. 4 (1991): 589–604; A. G. Wright, "The Widow's Mite: Praise or Lament?—A Matter of Context," *Catholic Biblical Quarterly* 44 (1982): 256–65.

39. Von Campenhausen, *Tradition and Life*, 101.

40. J. D. G. Dunn, "Jesus and Purity: An Ongoing Debate," *New Testament Studies* 48 (2002): 465.

41. Dietmar Neufeld, "Jesus' Eating Transgressions and Social Impropriety in the Gospel of Mark: A Social Scientific Approach," *Biblical Theology Bulletin* 30 (2000): 21. See Bruce J. Malina, *Christian Origins and Cultural Anthropology: Practical Models for Biblical Interpretation* (Atlanta, GA: John Knox Press, 1986).

42. Neufeld, "Jesus' Eating Transgressions," 21.

43. Von Campenhausen, *Tradition and Life*, 105.

44. Carolyn Osiek and David L. Balch, *Families in the New Testament World: Households and House Churches*, Family, Religion and Culture Series (Louisville, KY: Westminster John Knox Press, 1997).

45. Von Campenhausen, *Tradition and Life*, 108.

46. Ibid., 105.

47. John Painter, "When Is a House Not Home? Disciples and Family in Mark 3:13-35," *New Testament Studies* 45 (1999): 512. See also Ernest Best, *Disciples and Discipleship*, chap. 4 on the family of Jesus.

48. Vaage, "An Other Home," 752.

49. Ibid., 744, 755.

50. Ibid., 756.

51. Goehring, "Asceticism," 105.

52. Ware, "The Way of the Ascetics," in Wimbush and Valantasis, *Asceticism*, 13.

53. Valantasis,"Constructions," 795.

54. Ibid., 796.

55. Ibid., 799.

56. Stephen J. Patterson, "Askesis and the Early Jesus Tradition" in Vaage and Wimbush, *Asceticism and the New Testament*, 49.

57. Ibid., 65.

58. David F. Watson, "The *Life of Aesop* and the Gospel of Mark: Two Ancient Approaches to Elite Values," *Journal of Biblical Literature* 129, no. 4 (2010): 714.

59. Dunn, "Jesus and Purity," 449–67.

60. Ibid., 463.

61. John Donahue, "Tax Collectors and Sinners," *Catholic Biblical Quarterly* 33, no. 1 (1971): 39–61.

62. See Charles N. Giblin, " 'The Things of God' in the Question Concerning Tribute to Caesar," *Catholic Biblical Quarterly* 33 (1971): 510–13.

63. S. S. Bartchy, "Table Fellowship," in DJG, 796–800; Kathleen E. Corley, *Private Women, Public Meals, Social Conflict in the Synoptic Tradition* (Peabody, MA: Hendrickson, 1993); Bruce J. Malina, *The New Testament World: Insights from Cultural Anthropology* (Louisville, KY: Westminster John Knox Press, 1993); Jerome H. Neyrey, "Meals, Food, and Table Fellowship," in *The Social Sciences and New Testament Interpretation*, ed. Richard Rohrbaugh (Peabody, MA: Hendrickson, 1996), 159–82.

64. Neufeld, "Jesus' Eating Transgressions," 16.

65. Ibid., 20.

66. Elizabeth S. Malbon, "Fallible Followers: Women and Men in the Gospel of Mark," *Semeia* 28 (1983): 29–48.

67. Ibid., 41.

68. Bonnie B. Thurston, *Preaching Mark* (Minneapolis, MN: Fortress Press, 2002), chap. 7, and *The Spiritual Landscape of Mark* (Collegeville, MN: Liturgical Press, 2008), chap. 5.

69. Sharyn E. Dowd, *Prayer, Power, and the Problem of Suffering Mark 11:22-25 in the Context of Markan Theology* (Atlanta, GA: Scholars Press, 1988).

70. In"The Religious Authorities in the Gospel of Mark" (*New Testament Studies* 36 [1990]: 42–65), J. D. Kingsbury suggests Mark's portrayal of the religious authorities is not historical but polemical. We are to understand them as representatives of opposition to Jesus. See Elizabeth Struthers Malbon, "The Jewish Leaders in the Gospel of Mark: A Literary Study of Marcan Characterization," *Journal of Biblical Literature* 108, no. 2 (1989): 259–81.

71. John Paul Heil, "The Narrative Strategy and Pragmatics of the Temple Theme in Mark," *Catholic Biblical Quarterly* 59, no. 1 (1997): 98–99. See also Clinton Wahlen, "The Temple in Mark and Contested Authority," *Biblical Interpretation* 15 (2007): 248–67.

72. Robert Gundry, *Mark: A Commentary on His Apology for the Cross* (Grand Rapids, MI: Eerdmans, 1993).

73. Bruce Malina, "Pain, Power and Personhood: Ascetic Behavior in the Ancient Mediterranean," in Wimbush and Valantasis, *Asceticism*, 162.

74. Ibid., 163, 167–68.

75. Morna D. Hooker, *Not Ashamed of the Gospel: New Testament Interpretations of the Death of Christ* (Grand Rapids, MI: Eerdmans, 1994), 141.

76. John R. Donahue, "Jesus as the Parable of God in the Gospel of Mark," *Interpretation* 32, no. 4 (1978): 386.

77. Valantasis, "Constructions of Power," 812.

78. Derrett, *The Ascetic Discourse*, 96.

79. For a contemporary reflection on this point, see Bonnie Thurston, "Iona: Icon of Marginality and Engagement," *The Coracle* 4 (Summer 2011): 9–10.

80. Watson, "The *Life of Aesop*," 715–16.

81. Anthony L. Saldarini, "Asceticism in the Gospel of Matthew," in Vaage and Wimbush, *Asceticism and the New Testament*, 22.

82. Mary Ann Tolbert, "Asceticism and Mark's Gospel," in Vaage and Wimbush, *Asceticism and the New Testament*, 40.

83. Ibid., 44–45.

84. Eduard Schweizer, "The Portrayal of the Life of Faith in the Gospel of Mark," *Interpretation* 32, no. 4 (1978): 387–99.

85. Vaage, "An Other Home," 758, 760.

86. Stephen P. Ahearne-Kroll, "Audience Inclusion and Exclusion as Rhetorical Technique in the Gospel of Mark," *Journal of Biblical Literature* 129, no. 4 (2010): 735.

87. Patterson, "Askesis," 65.

88. Vaage, "An Other Home," 744.

Epilogue

1. Nick Cave, "A Punk Rocker's Angry Christ," *Harper's Magazine* 297, no. 1783 (December 1998): 33. The material is excerpted from Cave's introduction to the Gospel according to Mark published by Grove Press in 1999.

2. Ibid., 34.

3. I confess to being so out of the mainstream that the first time I was asked this question after a talk, I was momentarily stunned, unable to make a connection between my lecture and Chinese food, the only "take-away" with which I was familiar.

4. Cave, "A Punk Rocker's Angry Christ," 33.

5. Ibid., 34.

6. Thomas H. Green, *When the Well Runs Dry: Prayer Beyond the Beginnings* (Notre Dame, IN: Ave Maria Press, 1979), 58–59.

7. Ibid., 59.

8. Ibid.

9. Stephen P. Ahearne-Kroll, "Audience Inclusion and Exclusion as Rhetorical Technique in the Gospel of Mark," *Journal of Biblical Literature* 129 (2010): 734–35.

10. Cave, 34.

11. Quoted in *Give Us This Day* 2, no. 7 (July 2012): 165, from Hans Urs von Balthasar, *Light of the Word* (San Francisco, CA: Ignatius Press, 1993), 219.

12. Mary Ann Tolbert, "Asceticism and Mark's Gospel," in Leif E. Vaage and Vincent L. Wimbush, *Asceticism and the New Testament* (New York/London: Routledge, 1999), 40.

13. Ibid., 45.

14. Deitmar Neufeld, "Jesus' Eating Transgressions and Social Impropriety in the Gospel of Mark: A Social Scientific Approach," *Biblical Theology Bulletin* 30 (2000): 20.

15. Tolbert, "Asceticism and Mark's Gospel," 40.

16. Leif E. Vaage, "An Other Home: Discipleship in Mark as Domestic Asceticism," *Catholic Biblical Quarterly* 71 (2009): 743.

17. Words by Percy Dearmer.

18. Mary Katharine Deeley, "Jesus, Disturber of the Peace," *Give Us This Day* 2, no. 7 (July 2012): 176.

19. Vaage, "An Other Home," 761. Even Matthew's magi return to "their own country *by another road*." (Matt 2:12, italics mine.)

20. For a full exposition of this perceptive and compelling idea, see A. T. Lincoln, "The Promise and the Failure: Mark 16:8," *Journal of Biblical Literature* 108 (1989): 283–300.

21. For more on this, see Bonnie Thurston, "Faith and Fear in Mark's Gospel," *The Bible Today* 23, no. 5 (September 1985): 305–10.